## Also by BRETT RUTHERFORD
### POETRY
Songs of the I and Thou (1968)
City Limits (1970)
The Pumpkined Heart: Pennsylvania Poems (1973, 2012)
Thunderpuss: In Memoriam (1987)
Prometheus on Fifth Avenue (1987, 2018)
At Lovecraft's Grave (1988)
In Chill November (1990)
Poems from Providence (1991, 2011)
Twilight of the Dictators (with Pieter Vanderbeck) (1992, 2009)
Knecht Ruprecht, or the Bad Boy's Christmas (1992)
The Gods As They Are, On Their Planets (2005, 2012, 2018)
Things Seen in Graveyards (2007, 2017)
Doctor Jones and Other Terrors (2008)
Anniversarius: The Book of Autumn (1984, 1986, 1996, 2011)
An Expectation of Presences (2012)
Trilobite Love Song (2014)

### PLAYS
Night Gaunts: An Entertainment Based on the Life and Work
of H.P. Lovecraft (1993, 2005)

### NOVELS
Piper (with John Robertson) (1985, 2018)
The Lost Children (1988, 2018)

### AS EDITOR/PUBLISHER
May Eve: A Festival of Supernatural Poems (1975)
Last Flowers: The Romance Poems of Edgar Allan Poe
and Sarah Helen Whitman (1987, 2003, 2008, 2011)
M.G. Lewis's Tales of Wonder. Annotated edition. (2010, 2012)
A.T. Fitzroy. Despised and Rejected. Annotated edition. (2010)
Death and the Downs: The Poetry of Charles Hamilton Sorley.
Annotated edition (2010, 2017)
Tales of Terror: The Supernatural Poem Since 1800
2 vols (2015-2016)

# CRACKERS AT MIDNIGHT

### NEW POEMS & REVISIONS 2015-2017

## BRETT RUTHERFORD

The Poet's Press

PITTSBURGH, PA

*Copyright © 2018 by Brett Rutherford*
*All Rights Reserved*

*The author places this work in the Public Domain
on January 1, 2030.*

Rev 1.1

ISBN 0-922558-95-7

*This is the 236th publication of*
**THE POET'S PRESS**
2209 Murray Avenue #3/ Pittsburgh, PA 15217
www.poetspress.org

# TABLE OF CONTENTS

Autumn Dragged Screaming (Anniversarius XLI)   9
In Chill November (Anniversarius XXV)   11
Autumn of the Oligarchs (Anniversarius XLII)   14
Arabesques on the State of Liberty   16
At the Tomb of Leonardo da Vinci   20
The Exhumation of Goethe   25
The Midnight Walks of Eben Byers   28
The Isolate Stone   33
The Dresser in Emily's Bedroom   35
One Night in Cyprus, 1974   36
Dead Princess   38
Snofru the Mad   39
Mrs. Friedman's Golem   42
Crackers at Midnight   54
Night Walker   55
Eldorado   57
New Year's Day   60
The Owl   63

TABLEAUX FROM A PENNSYLVANIA VILLAGE
   I. Cloud Actors   66
   II. The Bats At Dusk, The Clouds Withdraw   67
   III. War of the Lake Against Its Borders   65
   IV. Stormy Day in Spring   71

Lethe   72
Motherhood   74
Wartime Fragment   75
Nero and the Flamingo   76
Dreamers   79
Who Can Be A Poet All of the Time?   80
Swan Lake Variations   83
Lines Overheard at the Russian Tearoom   87
Variations on the Ibis   89
The Company of an Eagle   93
Frontier   96
Thwarted   98
Please, No   100
Wooing   101
The Loved Dead   102

Necropolis 106
Poets in a Chelsea Brownstone 108
Chaucer's Prologue to *The Parliament of Fowles* 110

ABOUT THE POEMS 119

ABOUT THE POET 124

ABOUT THIS BOOK 125

# CRACKERS AT MIDNIGHT

# ANNIVERSARIUS XLI: AUTUMN DRAGGED SCREAMING

So where is Autumn?
   It is the week of Halloween
      and — nothing.
The maples are green, oaks green,
   willows even greener,
pines frowning their drooping arms
as if to say, get on with it, already —
the drama is long past over.
Bird flocks rehearse their southern pilgrimage
   but come right back
to feast anew on unchilled worm and beetle.
Damp rain sogs down,
   slime mold slides silently
      onto and up the rotting beech trunk.
Mushrooms proliferate
   at an illicit rate.
The spiders are working overtime,
   harvestmen in jitter-skitter,
a Macy's parade of Daddy-Long-Legs.
Sparrows engorged, squirrels spherical
   with acorn overflow,
eat all and bury nothing.
And the flowers just keep on,
   well, flowering.
Only the birches are shivering,
reading truly the Northern Lights,
the wisping fall of Orionid meteors,
white trunk flagpoles alert, on edge,
expectant pencils stuck in the ground.
It might have gone on this way:
   Indian October
      into Mexican November,
into a luridly Amazon December.
Today the unseasonable yucca plant,
   tomorrow the writhing anaconda!

It might have gone on,
    had not a thirteen-foot truck,
somewhere just south of Pittsburgh,
slid under an eleven-foot overpass,
the top peeled off like a sardine can.

One dull brown oak-leaf escaped it,
    and then a torrent
of sumac and willow, locust and maple,
    an Arctic air blast,
dust-devils, the choking lung-clot
    of burning leaf-piles.

And as the oblivious driver
    went southward, southerly, south,
intending to take the autumn hostage,
instead he cracked the heavens open.
The horizon turned yellow instantly,
    the soft green lap of leaves
became the crackle-crisp
chatter of Rattatosk,
    the Vikings' gossip squirrel.
Up, up Ygdrassil the World Ash
the singe of Autumn rose up.

Red now the long carpet in maple grove,
fiery the brush-fire burn of euonymous,
yellow the leaf-sky in azure tracery.

Come winter, then, if you must,
    come autumn *now,*
a world-held breath of defiance.

I go, I go, a leaf, in glory.

# ANNIVERSARIUS XXV: IN CHILL NOVEMBER

> The leaves be red,
> The nuts be brown,
> They hang so high
> They will not fall down.
> —*Elizabethan Round, Anon.*

The snow has come.
The leaves have fallen.
Long nights commit the chill
low sun and flannel clouds cannot disperse.
We walk the park, stripped now
    to mere schematics,
vision drawn out to farther hills
now that the forest is blanked
like flesh turned glass on X-ray negative.

These woods are sham so near the solstice,
play out a murder mystery of birch and maple.
The riddle is, who's dead and who's pretending?

That witches' elm with clinging broomsticks —
    is it deceased, or somnolent?
Which of these trees will never bloom again:
    a Lombardy poplar stripped by blight—
    a maple picked clean by gypsy moths —
    a thunder-blasted pedestal of ash —
    a moribund sycamore whose only life
        came in a few vain buds
            (growing like dead men's hair and nails,
            slow to acknowledge the rot below)?
The ground is a color cacophony,
    alive, alive!
the treeline a study in gray and brown.

So, who can tell
    the bare tree from the dead,
    the thin man from the skeleton?
Which denizens of wood-lot shed these leaves?
Which is a corpse? a zombie?
Which one is but a vermin shell?
Which treads the night on portable roots,
    festooned with bats,
    sinking its web of trailing vines
    into the veins of saplings?
Which stalwart oaks will topple,
which trunks cave in to termite nests?
Which is the next victim of carpenter ants?
How can we tell the living from the dead?

It is just the month: November lies.
    October always tells the truth.
You could no more fake
    the shedding of leaves
than simulate a pulse in stone.

Only the living fall in love,
only the living cry for joy,
only the living relinquish *that* month
in red and yellow shuddering!

The pines,
    those steeple-capped Puritans,
what price their ever-green?
Scrooge trees, they hoard their summers,
withhold their foliage,
refuse to give the frost its due.

Ah, they are prudent,
    Scotch pine and wily cedar,
    touch-me-not fir and hemlock.
They will live to a ripe old age
(if you can call that living).

I shun this sham Novembering.
Turn back the calendar: there, Halloween,
no, further back to the start of leaf-fall!
There! The first-frost autumn shuddering!

Love! Burn! Sing! Crumble!
Dance! Wind! Fall! Tumble
into the wind-blown pyramid of leaves!
Spin in a whirling dust-devil waltz!
Leaf-pile! Treetops! Tramping on clouds!
Weightless, flying, red-caped October!

# ANNIVERSARIUS XLII: AUTUMN OF THE OLIGARCHS

*Come September,*
those dirty brown oak leaves,
tumbling around like homeless persons,
are not acceptable here.
Oak-leaf clusters, preserved and dried
in tones of cheerful red and orange
will make a suitable display
for our early-harvest luncheon.
The noise is worth it — those tawny Mexicans
leaf-blowing till every last derelict
of maple and birch, alder and sycamore
are hosed and bagged, and tucked away —
worth it to have a picture-perfect lawn
neat as a golf course.

*Come October,*
and every last leaf will be gone.
The acorns shall have been harvested,
bird-nests removed.
Those pine cones falling like hand-grenades:
one can scarcely keep up with them,
but go they must. The traps shall be set
for the aberrant beaver, the rabbit,
the ever-destructive mole.
As for the birds, the Ornithology Club
has come up with an "approved" list —
the drones, with rifle-shots, will cull the rest.
All of our poorer relatives patrol the woods
for deer and fox and all unwanted mammals.
The Approved Cat and her progeny, keep clear
the house and grounds of rats, and mice, and voles.
As for the squirrels — anarchists all! — we make
their lives a misery with a pack of Approved Hounds

until we find a way to breed those rodents sterile
(a break-through that will come in handy
as we down-size — just think,
a whole continent all for the taking, all over again,
but I get ahead of myself —)

*Come November,*
the green turf, the stripped-bare trees
    like telephone poles,
the grounds secure, the fences electrified,
we'll settle in for the fall and winter.
There will be inconveniences, of course.
Next to the martini, an iodine tablet.
The New York jaunts a thing of the past,
Old Master paintings all moved to a solid bunker
(best of the Met slipped out by sleight-of-hand);
the dinosaurs and those quaint old dioramas
of Arctic and African species (fakes all in Manhattan
as long ago we stealthed away the originals).
Deep in a cave we have the best of the best
and we can visit any time, on trips to the vaults
where we've moved all our solid assets.
When things calm down, the missiles spent
and the Geiger-counter clicks are down to drip-drop;
when the cities are cleansed and the suburbs leveled —
just you wait for the turkey day to end all turkey days.
Done by Thanksgiving next, the generals assured us,
just the one percent (us) and about five percent (them),
the ones we chose. By God, we'll have stuffing,
cigars and brandy by the fireplace, a starry night.

*Come December,*
sure as hell it'll be a White Christmas.

# ARABESQUES ON THE STATUE OF LIBERTY

1
Bad Dingo rides
the Staten Island ferry
dusk till dawn,
clinging to rail,
nestling an all-night
tumescence,
hard at the sight
of the robed lady,
vast,
unapproachable.

He's stalking her,
biding his time.
Some night
   there'd be a fog,
   a power failure.
He'd come up behind her,
   prodding the small
   of her spine
with his imperious knife,
jostling her bronze buttocks
with his ardent flesh prod.
She'd drop the tablet;
   the torch would sputter.
He'd push her off her pedestal.
Bad Dingo would give it to her good
   the way he did to all the white ladies
   in parks and stairwells and subway cars.
This would be the rape of all rapes,
   the pinnacle of his career,
      the ultimate boast
"See that toppled goddess
   in the harbor--
she ain't so proud now
since someone had her,

made her moan.
Bad Dingo had her,
    stuck it to the Statue,
white lady Liberty!"

2
In Chinatown,
Mrs. Wang mounts
a quiet rebellion
against the ways of the elders.

She has done all
her mother asked her:
married the boy
   the matchmaker ordained,
bore sons and daughters
   in regular order
burned joss and incense
   at every altar,
      sending ghost gold and peaches,
         phantom cars and televisions
            Hong Kong Hell dollars
               to the teeming, greedy dead.

Now her husband travels,
   has mistresses, won't talk
      about his gambling.
Her children are gone,
   married to foreign devils.
Her round-eyed grandchildren
      won't learn Mandarin,
      will never send joss riches
      her way when she is dead.

Now she becomes a whirlwind:
She sells her jade and porcelain,
cleans out her savings account,
buys an airline ticket
for San Francisco —
from there, who knows?

She pawns the statuette
of pearly white Kuan-Yin,
the Goddess of Mercy
whose only blessing
was endless childbirth
and washing and ironing,

On a whim she buys another
to take its place at her bedside:
a foot-high Statue of Liberty
with batteries and glowing torch.

She leaves it for her husband,
her wedding ring
on its spiky crown.

*3*
Today two New York titans
switch places.

A grumpy green Liberty
strides up Fifth Avenue,
crushing pedestrians in verdigris.
Her sandaled feet
send buses flying,
kiosks shattering.

Her great head turns
among the office towers.
She reaches in,
pulls screaming executives
through razor-edge panes,
undresses them
with her copper fingers,
discards them one by one
to the pavement
twenty stories below.

The man she wants
is not among them. He's got
to be a real American,
one of those Arrow shirt models,
blond, and a screamer,
a yielding but unwilling male
under her stern metallic nails.
The more he cries out, *Put me down*,
the more she likes him.

Uptown, she finds him:
a tousle-headed messenger,
scooped up from his bicycle.
She cups him in one palm,
drops her tablet,
rolls up her sleeves,
and starts the painful ascent
of the Empire State Building.

Downtown
on Liberty Island,
King Kong wields a torch,
incinerates all passing freighters,
capsizes the passenger ships.
He hurls great boulders skyward,
picks off incoming airplanes one by one.
*He* is guarding the harbor now.
*He* is a real American
and he shouts his slogans:
*America First.*
*Stay out.*
*Go home.*
*No foreigners allowed.*

# AT THE TOMB OF LEONARDO DA VINCI

*At the Chapel of Saint Hubert, Amboise, France*

*1*
Whose bones are these, beneath a slab inscribed
with the name of Leonardo? Not all
is right, for the *fleur-de-lys* floor tiles run
upside-down around the graven tomb-slab,
and the whole affair is sideways, transept

in a cramped chapel, a mausoleum
to Titan genius into which gods —
the three-in-one Ghost, the *Bon Dieu*
    and the ever-bleeding Jesus —
have intruded, demanding obeisance.
Who comes to kneel, kneels at the wrong altar.

Leonardo sleeps not in Italy.
Long was his exile from native Florence;
his neglect under the scheming Sforzas,
ignominy among the courtiers
and silks of ever-wavering Milan;
Rome's bitter rivalries, amid the glare
of Rafael and Michelangelo,
world's capital not big enough for three.

So his (or someone's) skeleton sleeps here
in the pale white light and lull of the Loire.
Here, once, he had a house — a tunnel led
from chateaux to work-room, so sly Francis,
fretting over his unfettered brilliance
could visit him without a by-your-leave,
the King of France and he, of Science and Art,
in long consults and colloquies, royal
nose and narrow eyes above the arm
and the stooped shoulder that drew,
drew endlessly and wrote in an unknown script.

What has Saint Hubert, with bow and horn,
the patron of deranged hunters, to do with him,
the scribbling guest beneath the floor-slab?
The spire is spiked with antlery, façade
with cross-bearing stag and hound and falcon;
at every turn a discordant gargoyle
agape with medieval gossip and spite.
Why not carve winged flight to the distant peaks,
or the gears and wheels of great water-works?

Why not stained glass to the glory of Man,
the unfurled secrets of veins,
the idea-causeway through nerve to cranium,
his decades' study of anatomy,
robot and catapult and helical gear,
the secrets of wending winds and sun-rays?

No one, it seems, had ever intended this,
a Gothic tomb for a Renaissance god.
Another tomb housed him, another chapel
leveled to rubble by angry peasants,
raided for building stone by Bonaparte.
And from that ruin and a scrabble-yard
of broken bone and tombstone fragments,
they sought to re-assemble da Vinci.

Which one was him? Look, there! No, over there!
Bring a light! The one with the largest skull!
Would not that intellectual brow and brain
require an enormous head to hold them?
And there, that long humerus and radius:
make sure to find a matching pair for all.
Are those the metacarpals and finger bones
that painted the Mona Lisa? Yes, those!
Two hundred and six bones to collect
to assemble a complete da Vinci.

Did they get them all? Did they get enough?
Are there mixed in some trace of whore or jester,
some simpering cardinal or king's mistress?
They did their best. Napoleon the Third
approved and blessed the new interment,
and France, once more, had its Italian.

Corpse or *corpus*, which matters most?
Nothing will ever awaken here, nor look
askance at his mis-matched hands,
or grimace at unfamiliar incisors.
The *corpus* of an artist is his art.

Twenty-one paintings survive, our treasure.
Ten thousand notebook pages —Melzi's hoard
for a scant half-century — as many
as a hundred thousand drawings upon
the densely-populated pages, cut up
to frame and sell the sketches, the writing
discarded, till half of his work was lost.
Five thousand pages of notes have come to us —
waited four hundred years to be published.
Only now do we know half of his words,
the body of Leonardo your hand
can hold and leaf through, mind to mind.

Whose bones these are, beneath the *fleur-de-lys*
flagstones of St. Hubert's — who knows, or cares?
Da Vinci: your real winged self shall join us
upon the long, and cold, and lonely flight
to the far side of the bright field of stars.

# THE EXHUMATION OF GOETHE

*East Germany, 1970*

By all means do this at night, while Weimar
sleeps, while even those whose job it is to watch
the watchers, sleep. In merciful dark,
the third-shift silence when the local electric plant
shuts down for the Good of the State,

take a cart — no, not a car,
    a hand-drawn cart —
dampen its wheels so your journeys to,
    and from, and back
to the foggy graveyard are soundless.

Do not awaken the burghers!
Here are the keys to the wrought-iron gates —
mind you don't rattle them.
The crypt has been purposefully left unlocked.
You need but draw the door.
The cart will just squeeze through
(Engineer Heinrich has measured everything!)

Open the sarcophagus as quietly as possible.
Watch the fingers! Don't leave a mark
on the hand-carved cover.
Be sure it's Goethe, the one with a "G."
We don't want his crypt-mate Schiller
(too many anti-People tendencies).

Lift up the whole thing gently.
The bones will want to fly apart.
Only the shroud, and some mummified meat
keep him in the semblance of skeleton.
Just scoop the whole thing up
like a pancake, then into the cart.

Here's a bag for the skull. Don't muss
those ash-gray laurel leaves.
We plan to coat them in polymer
after we study that Aryan skull
whose brain conceived of Faust,
Egmont, and sorrowful Werther.
We're going to wire the bones together,
strip off that nasty flesh,
maybe bleach him a little,
make a respectable ghost of Goethe.

Who knows, if he looks good enough,
in a newly-lined sarcophagus,
we could put him on display.
Come to *Kulturstadt*!
See Goethe's body!
Even better than Lenin!
(Can we say that?)

It will be a world attraction.
We'll pipe in lieder and opera.
Tour guides will be dressed as Gretchen.
Maybe a fun house
with Mephistopheles,
a sausage-fest at Brander's Inn.

Ah! the cart is here! The bones,
yes, the bones. Unfortunate, the odor.
We can work on that.
The colors, *mein Gott*,
(excuse the expression)
they will not please —
over there, Klaus,
   if you're going to be sick —

It's such a *little* skeleton —
was he really so short?
The books said he towered
over his contemporaries.

So much for the books!
And the shroud — that color —
not at all what we imagined.
Perhaps the opera house
could make a new one.

Watch those ribs —
so many little bones
in the fingers.
Things are just not . . .
holding together.

I can't do this.
The project is canceled.
Poets are just too — flimsy.
Put this mess back
where it came from.
Next time let's exhume a general,
Bismarck, the Kaiser,
someone with a sword and epaulets.
Armor would be even better.
*The People want giants!*

# THE MIDNIGHT WALKS OF EBEN BYERS

Grand cemetery, Pittsburgh's Allegheny,
arcs up to a hilltop, where nestled
in a millionaires' necropolis, stands one,
a perfect replica of a Doric temple,
a steel magnate's mausoleum. Sunlit,
Dryads seem to converge upon it,
a timeless Aegean day-dream.
Moonlit, it is the uneasy prison
of what remains of Eben Byers. Its stolid doors,
which might try two men's strength to wedge
them open to a peeping-gap, are weighted
so that a tiny push from inwards hurls
them open. The dark inside is palpable
and seems to thrust back against you.
One casket there is lined with lead, they say —
pallbearers once groaned to lift and lower it
from catafalque to hearse to wall-niche.
This one, amid the disapproving Byers dead,
somehow broke loose of a Gordian knot
of iron chains and adamantine padlocks,
undid the patient webwork of melancholic spiders,

and floats, a log on a stream of unseen plasma,
to any place its never-sleeping occupant desires.
Police reports of a roaming black casket are filed
under "Hoaxes," "Pranks" and "Hallucinations."

A roaming casket is bad enough. But when
it parks itself on a cemetery by-lane
and its occupant takes shape from smoke-mist —
now that is the stuff of madness.
How he emerges from his lead encasement —
whether the lid creaks up on rusted hinges,
or whether he oozes out from a mouse-hole
it took him long years to scratch out — no one knows.
Once out, he mostly walks the graveyard,
striding among the oaks and sycamores.
Nocturnal deer and 'possums flee him
as his heavy tramp cracks pavement
and the flap of his metallic shroud dulls
the night-chants of frog and cicada.

His gelid eyes still water in their sockets;
there is flesh still, though dead since 1932,
on the withered left hand, palm upward
to scan the heavens for sustenance:
for rest assured, that whatever walks,
is hungry. If you scale the fence, you might
just find him on the Butler Street down-slope,
amid a cluster of erectile obelisks. Long years
he watched from there, and no one saw him,
until the last mill died, until the flicker-fire
no longer red-glazed the tombed hillside.
It is said that he is slightly lumin-
escent, that a greenish glow clings
to his felt hat-tip with corpse-hair aureole,
that arcs of small lightning or St. Elmo's Fire
emit from his bony fingertips.

He runs his good hand on every granite
marker, not reading inscriptions, no:
he feels the butterfly flow of gamma rays
from thorium, sniffs the good whiffs of radon
that please him more than he can say.

To those who have seen him, and not
died screaming, he is known as "Radium Man."
The steel mill he inherited was less to him
than travel and a good game of golf,
which he played to champion. Let others
build opera houses, if only he could outdo
the rest of the magnate class on the course.
And he did: '06 U.S. Amateur. Until the pain,
his right arm a misery of knotted nerve-fire.
A Yale man, he trusted a Harvard man,
who, bottling the famed success of the cure,
the radium-and-water treatment of Europe,
offered him a sample of Radiothor.
The ultimate in pep and healing, its label said,
*This is the cure for the living dead.*

By damn, one bottle and he was good as new.
He told friends, and pretty soon the Mayor
of Pittsburgh had drunk a hundred bottles.
There was talk around the leather-chaired club
of renewed and superhuman bedroom feats.
Radiothor came in by the carload.
If one bottle was good, and a hundred
turned Milquetoast into a roaring Don Juan,
why not three bottles a day?
Are we not entitled to the most of the best?

Eben Byers drank fourteen hundred bottles
of Radiothor. In the ensuing collapse and
galloping cancers, parts of his skull gave way
and his jaw ripped free and fell to the floor.
When they darkened the room where his corpse lay
it did not stay dark — his teeth and nails
glowed greenish, and what was left of hair

waved of its own accord like tided seaweed.
His lead-lined coffin made national headlines.
Then silence. Then a decade of the sleep of death.
But radium lived on with its 1600-year half-life;
it forged a new alliance with bone, neuron, sinew, joint.
When atom bombs erupted, his eyes widened.
When Strontium 90 fallout dusted down,
his dry tongue licked his upper canines, craving.
When isotopes lit the hospital skyline, when X-rays
arc'd on and off like fireworks, he sensed, and knew
there was more of what he craved, things new
to the Periodic Table he could one day savor.
When, at a nearby research institute
a pilot breeder reactor created Plutonium,
he knew it was time to set himself in motion.

The thing that walks at midnight, down
from its Doric resting place, is not content
with holding his hand out beggar-like —
for what? Dim manna of the night sky,
massless neutrinos passing through,
the taunting wave-pulse of a magnetar,
the warm hum of cosmic rays,
and just before dawn banishes him to hiding,
the hot half-sun at horizon, a Cyclops eye
from infra red to gamma beaming.
Radium Man wants more.
His left hand clenches, unclenches
as he thinks about the possible feasts
he might have at Chernobyl, quake-
shaken Fukishima, even Three-Mile Island.
His heirs would interfere, or seek
a discreet disinterment and cremation;
the servants who did what he asked
unquestioned, are dead and buried — sad
to say, permanently dead and buried.
He is alone in this. And all he can manage
to utter now, with his truncated face,
is a kind of *hunh* …… *hunh* ….. *hunh*
to the owls and bats and ravens.

Once in a while, his bad arm rises,
an involuntary wave of *what's-the-use
anyway-you're-dead-now?*
Pray you do not see it,
if you chance to come upon him
by his Doric mausoleum
with its gaping-open doors —
or from his casket rising god knows
how far afield from Lawrenceville.

No other spectre, be sure, is like him.
Beware the skeletal right hand
that holds aloft, as club or cudgel,
the jawbone of Eben Byers.

# THE ISOLATE STONE

*Mary, Mary, quite contrary,*
*how does your garden grow?*
In the unkempt high grass
of North Burial Ground,
the isolate stone affronts
the eye in long-shadowed autumn.
Mary of no family,
unChristianed of surname,
were you housemaid, spinster,
unmentioned attic-dweller
of uncertain parentage?
Why nameless here, unparented,
brotherless and sisterless,
childless most certainly?
Except that she loved someone
we nothing know of Mary.
Did she attend *his* wedding,
silent over the vow he made her,
ruing the treasure she gave him
that a woman can give but once?
Did she pace his street nightly
eyeing the windows bright,
more of them each year as child
after child that were his but not hers
emerged to world conquering?
Did her rival know she even existed?
Is his grave nearby? Is that it?
Does her accusing stone face *his* now
so that every dawning confronts him,
and her rival, rotting oblivious
in the ground beside him —
Mary tomb-staring them, forever and a day?
She gets the best view of him,
the sunlit brow of his monument
always in view of hers.

Only the tall grass, untrimmed,
obscures her view in the high summer.

In this stone a whole story,
a life of abnegation and wanting.
She waits for its telling one day
leaving one clue for everyone
in stone-cutter's script.
She chose the plot, she stood
with the neatly-sketched letters
as she ordered the stone,
eyeing the angles between
*his* and *hers* and *mine*.

*Mary, Mary quite contrary*,
your stone says only

BROKEN-HEARTED
MARY.

# THE DRESSER IN EMILY'S BEDROOM

Right there, feet from the bed she died in,
were the poems, sewn up in tiny fascicle bundles,
unread, not to be read, not to be published,
monoprint chapbooks arranged and re-
arranged to suit intended readers
she was too reticent to address,
ever, except from behind a door, ajar.
They came from *there*, her writing table
(no bigger than a *oiuja* board),
from planchette pen to folded leaf
stitched shut and mummy-wrapped,
living and smothering just feet from where
a gasp and pen-dab and a foot-tap
telegraphed them into being.
How many enwrapped, entombed inside
that oblong, moth-proof drawer?
how many survivors of admonition
*a poet should never ... a lady does not?*

Eighteen hundred tightly-wound mortars
she wryly called her "little hymns"
huddled like captives in a slave-hold,
sea-echoes lost in suffocated nautilus,
an unlit library with no borrowers —
how many silent nights did she browse there,
and turn the pages, and close them,
and push the drawer shut?

Emily Dickinson at Amherst,
I in your room as close to fainting
as ever in my adult existence,
at tear-burst, with a strangled cry I dare
not utter. A life, a life's work,
a soul's compression that one executor
could have tossed away for kindling,
or suppressed for jealousy or malice.
But we have you, Emily, we have you always,
your words in a fascicle of stitched stars.

# ONE NIGHT IN CYPRUS, 1974

On the back of a truck
hurtling without headlamps
on a moonlit night on Cyprus,
the archbishop sat, cross-legged.
He saw great silhouettes of cedar trees
and overhanging crags black-edged,
an open sky of fierce and unnamed stars —
or stars whose names he'd never learned,
though Greek and Arab astronomers
had classed and ordered them,
hard-tracing beasts and maidens,
hunters and bears, cup-bearers loyal
to the rampant, seducing cosmos,
now a mere tapestry for Christ's passing.
Now he, a mariner without sail or star
had put his trust in strangers (strangers
who came from god and might be god),
hidden like thief beneath a flapping tarp,
a lump among figs and onions
inhaling the incense of root-earth.
The driver stopped, the men
invisible to him in the truck cab
came 'round to lift the tarp. He winced.
*You may stretch your legs, Father.*
*We have reached the peak —*
*So far no sign of any soldiers.*
*We'll send a scout ahead on foot,*
*the crossroads below a last point*
*of danger we'll be stopped and captured.*
He nodded, thanked and blessed them,
his hand making the cross, the crossroads sign
as he thought of the feared places
where Hecate was summoned and fetuses
buried. Thus one always shuddered at crossroads.
He walked to road-edge. If ever a prayer
was called for, it was now. No altar, no walls.

The arched cedar tree cupped praying hands,
the slope was dotted with flowers —
what color, the asphodel at midnight?
He said some words, not for himself at first,
then for himself, for so much depended
on his getting out and away, to save the country.
But where, in dark night, did prayers go?

★ ★ ★

I never knew you. I never heard of you.
I have never seen Cyprus, and yet the dream
that seized me was realer than real.
I felt the pain of your bones, I sighed your sigh
as you knelt and prayed. I did not grasp the words
or the language in which they were uttered.
Yet my self watching myself dreaming told me:
this is Cyprus, and this is happening.
Your prayer, for whatever cause, rose not to heaven:
it came to me, an atheist, and half a world away.

You fled the Greek-led coup on Cyprus, a hunted man,
and you escaped that night; you flew to London.
You returned to endure a Turkish invasion,
your dream of one Cyprus for Greek and Turk alike
shattered by tanks and airplanes.
Your statue stands in Nicosia.
A hate line still divides your island.

Why you, why me, Archbishop Makarios?

# DEAD PRINCESS

Not huntress, but hunted,
    not chasing the antler'd stag
        but run down like the fallow doe —
not arrows, but flashbulb quivers
    felled you. Hands reached
        to seize your garlands,
    to tear some trophy
        from your dying.

Not princess, and not yet goddess —
    your temple is marble tomb,
        an island inaccessible.
Gamekeepers cross
    in a humble rowboat,
leave flowers for you
    as at an altar.

London becomes a pagan festival,
    where every living flower is cut
        and laid amid tears & sobbing
as if to affirm in desiccation
    that all must die,
        that bloom once cut
            is never resurrected,
no matter how many requiems.

Proud state that claimed permit from Jove
to trample the far horizon
calls now for this mere mortal
to be sublimed at once to a temple:
grave and grove and mourning day,
sacred to Diana.

# SNOFRU THE MAD

With a name like Snofru[1]
   you'd better be good
   as a Pharaoh, as a survivor.
Would the gods laugh, he wondered,
   when his weighing time came up —
   his heart against a feather
   on the fatal balance —
would tittering among them
make his recitation falter?

A careful planner,
he lays *four* boats in his pyramid,
one pointed in each direction —
he'd launch all four
so his soul could elude
the pursuing god Set
and confound old Ammit,
the Eater of the Dead.

Grave robbers? He'd baffle them,
build *three* great pyramids
   for Snofru the Pharaoh —
   hang the cost!
He'd bury an imposter
in each sarcophagus.
The gods alone would know
his final resting place,
a well-appointed tomb
whose architect he'd strangled.

---

[1] Snofru or Snefru was Pharaoh in the Fourth Dynasty and the immediate predecessor of Khufu (Cheops), builder of the Great Pyramid. Historians are baffled as to why Snofru built himself three separate pyramids.

As for his Queen Hetephras,
dead these three years now,
he left her innards
in an alabaster jar,
yet carried her mummy away.

Nights, he unwinds her wrappings,
kisses her natron-scented lips,
caresses her sewn-up belly,
then carefully restores
her royal bandages,
her mask and jewels.

His courtiers avoid him,
smell death despite
the unguents and incense.
An impudent general
already makes eyes
at his daughter. They scheme.
There is talk, there is talk.
He will neither make war, nor peace,
turns back ambassadors
as he spends his days divining
how to turn his eye-blink life
into the gods' eternity.

One night he slips away.
The upstart will assume his name,
bed his black-eyed daughter,
inherit his unused pyramid —
the better to advance his stratagem.

With pride and pomp
he circled his name[2]
on a hundred monuments,
but he is far from Memphis now,
where he speaks to his servants
in but a whisper.

---

[2] Snofru was the first Pharaoh to enclose his name in a cartouche.

His modest sarcophagus,
when that time comes,
is inscribed with another name.
His journey West
will be uneventful.

Then, coming and going
among the living the dead,
he'll watch as the proud
are judged and eaten,

then take his place, unsandaled,
plain as the commonest slave,
serving his mummy-bride
at the table of the gods.

# MRS. FRIEDMAN'S GOLEM

*i*
Because I was "the heathen boy" and smart
enough to pass for Jewish, free I ran
on the Friedmans' neighboring house and grounds.
One early-summer day, with Marilyn,
a year my elder, we played in the evergreens
that fringed their leaf-filled, empty swimming pool.
An endless ball of packing twine unwound
around the spindly trees, not spider webs,
but corridors and doorways, here a room,
a closet there — in an almost clearing
a wide space for a sunbeam-lit ballroom.
The hotel dubbed "The Sunny-Day-Only"—
the sleeping rooms and beds would be up above
in tree-house heights to be scaled by ladders.
As our fancy turned up to ziggurat
heights and bird-nest bedding, we didn't see
the bearded, smiling Mennonite preacher
until he was right upon us. "Children!"
he hailed us, then asked if we believed
in Jesus, who was up above the trees,
and died, so we could go to heaven too.
Up then went Marilyn's defiant chin.
"We're Jewish." He looked at me, dubious.
"And you?" he asked. I shrugged. "So what *are* you?" —
"I've never been in a church," I told him.
A pine cone fell at his feet and shattered.
"Don't you believe in anything?" he growled,
now in a tone that said grownup-to-child.
"Superman, maybe," I mocked him, and turned
to resume my arbor-building. He left
dumbfounded, his Anabaptist faith scorned
by children's string maze in a Druid grove.

Our string hotel survived two nights, then vanished.
"My mother told me the robins took it —"
so Marilyn explained it, " — for their nests.
Besides, the guests are coming. It's June now,
and the swimming season starts tomorrow."
The *season*, as we all came to know it,
was at the Friedmans' immense swimming pool;
by June's end swell, a half a hundred guests,
from wading toddlers to aquatic teens,
babies in prams to motionless elders,
umbrella-tabled at the green-blue pool.

That afternoon, indoors, we played at cards —
an outsize canasta with twenty decks,
which drew a great shriek from Mrs. Friedman
as she came home with the month's vast larder
of picnic food and frozen lemonade.
Our task: re-separate and sort the decks
and stack them up in a neat pyramid.
Summers these rumpled cards had seen before,
beneath the hawk-eyed ladies' gaze, enthroned
and clucking at their poolside card tables;
the cards would doubtless outlive some of them.

Scores would be there by shimmering August,
the men apart from the women, a cloud
of cigarettes where they leaned together
and worried over business and politics.
Children in bathing suits ran to and from
the house, wet trails and footprints to and from
the bathrooms, the sinks, the freezer. Sometimes
I was asked to take ice or a pitcher
to one of the tables, there where I learned
one should never swim just after eating
and tales of drowning and worries about
the unfortunates who got polio,
and Mrs. Friedman's oft-repeated fretting
about one bad boy who peed in the pool,
never enough chlorine when that occurs.

The men talked
   of other things I knew nothing of
      in a language I did not understand.


*ii*
"The season really starts next week, you see. *Next* week."
As Marilyn explained to me. "Mother has asked
everyone to come over tomorrow to help.
The pool needs cleaned, the cobwebbed furniture wiped down,
Dead leaves, dog poop and pine cones everywhere. We'll see
if anyone shows up." — "Won't they?" I asked. — "Not one."
Card sorting done, we went back to our comic books:
she read my *Superman*, I, her *Wonder Woman*,
a title no boy would ever be caught reading.

Saturday came. The day waned and one car only
came up the lane and parked. All day we made the ice
for grape juice and lemonade brimful in freezer
and buckets. Sandwiches were made, and snacks put out.
Squirrels came to the windows expectantly, bird-chirp
anticipated the crowd, the crumbs, the leavings.
I lingered for dinner as Mrs. Friedman seethed on,
serving cold plate with embarrassment and anger.
The guest was new, a stranger, a bearded, calm man
in a business suit they called Rabbi. His voice
was deep, and with a foreign sound I could not place.
"Rabbi Doctor Baruch," they said I should call him.
Already he knew my name, and turning, he said:
"And you are the little boy who is not Jewish
who made string Stars of David all over the porch
December last." I blushed, recalling Mrs. Friedman's
horror at finding her decorated house-front.
"He felt sorry for us," Mr. Friedman offered up,
"because we had no Christmas ornaments outside."
They all laughed heartily. Still no one would tell me
why my six-pointed ornaments had been torn down
with such speed and alarm. "Anyone driving by,"
was all that Marilyn's mother said, "they could see."

"But Rabbi," Mr. Friedman continued, "I know you wanted
to meet our friends." The rabbi shrugged. —
            "You call those friends?"
his wife retorted. "All summer long they come here,
they use the pool, we feed them, and pretend to laugh
at their worn-out humor. And all this work, for what?
I could be listening to the opera on the radio.
Not one of them will come and help us clean the pool!"

"So, next week I can come back," the Rabbi offered.
"All of us need to help Jews get out of Russia.
First Stalin was killing us all over again,
and now his heir, that smiling thug Khrushchev."
Mrs. Friedman had other worries:
"So who's going to clean the pool? Not you, Rabbi!
Shame on us if it came to that." Mr. Friedman
fussed with his sandwich and fork in embarrassment.
Silence and shadow-blink of a passing cloud held us.
The Rabbi's long-fingered hands passed twirling circles
twice in his dark beard, as though he had to ask it,
then, with one hand extended palm up he asked her,
"Mrs. Friedman, you want I should make a Golem?"

*iii*
Mouths opened wide, eyes wider.
Even I knew what a Golem was.
It was in *Famous Monsters*.
"A Golem," Mrs. Friedman gulped.
"Would it — could it — "
"Anything you want done, it can do.
It's not an easy thing, and I need not say
that no one should know afterwards.
I come from Poland, where such things are done."

The Rabbi turned an intense gaze on me.
"Boy, you are not Jewish?" —
                    "No, Rabbi, I'm not." —
"You are not Christian?" —
                    "No, I'm not." —
"Not even a tiny bit?" —

"I went two weeks to Bible School. They asked me
   not to come back." —
"So, you are not a Christian. Swear it." —
      I cleared my throat. Whatever this was,
         I had to be in on it.
"I swear I am not a Christian." —
"Never baptized?"
I knew what that was from movies.
                              "No, never baptized." —
"So, you do not know the secret name of God?"
      I could have said "Yahweh" or "Adonai," two words
         I already knew from poetry. Instead I said, "No." —

"Very well. You will be my assistant.
At ten o'clock, you come to the swimming pool. Tell no one."
I beamed from ear to ear. "I'll be there. I promise."

This was better than Christmas morning. A Golem. A Golem.
They sent me home. I crept to my bedroom.
A flashlight and comics would keep me awake.
At ten, I ran alongside the Friedman house. Two cars'
headlights full beamed on the swimming pool.
The Rabbi and Mr. Friedman were up the slope
that led to the scant woods above the property.
They stooped and touched bare ground.
"Strange clay, not like back home, but it will do,"
our sorcerer intoned, as with a walking stick
he outlined the lumpy shape of a man
on the bare and eroded clay hillside,
a place I knew, where owls and wild turkeys
lurked in the shrubs and saplings.
He passed his cane this way and that,
and uttering a prayer we could not-quite hear —
it seemed to hover an inch from his beard
like a will o'the wisp — a prayer not meant
for human ears but for spirits

And the shape he had outlined stood,
and separated itself from the yellow clay bank.

It stood. It shook itself free
of dust and tiny stones and tree-root.
It stood,
        and moved no further, inert
as a sculptor's first molding.
It was a lump with but a hint of legs,
arm-like extrusions bent at the elbow
and a great square head, two holes
where eyes should have been
and a mouth-gap the size of a mailbox.

Mr. Friedman pulled back in terror.
"I thought you were joking. I never thought.
My god, I never thought —"
Before I could react, the Rabbi had lifted me,
and placing a folded ribbon of paper
into my tiny hand, he put me up
on the Golem's forearm.

"Put the paper in the Golem's mouth.
Only then will he move
   and obey our orders."
I started to raise my left hand
to the horizontal gape
that was the Golem's mouth.
His beard brushed my ear
as he whispered, "Do not,
under any circumstances,
look into the Golem's eyes." —

"And what would happen, Rabbi?" —

"You would see things no one
was meant to see and live.
Just do as I ask and no more,
and you will be safe, and blessed."

My head averted, I found the mouth
by touch and slid the paper in.
There came a groan,

as low as a tuba in a July parade,
no, low as the bass drum that rattles
your stomach in passing,

and then I was standing,
the Rabbi's hand atop my head
for the longest time
until he let me go.

We saw the Golem in silhouette first
as the great shape lumbered
to the lit-up pool.
And so, with broom and mop
and chemicals, the hulking thing
descended the shallow-end stairs
into the vacant pool, as Mrs. Friedman,
at ease as though a local workman
were there before her, paced round
the pool and gave out orders.
*Sweep there, no, higher up,
you missed a spot.*

How long this took, I cannot recall.
Marilyn saw some of it
    from her bedroom window,
just lights and a shape in silhouette
and her mother going this way, that way
waving her arms in command.
(Her little sister, sent to bed early,
saw nothing.)

The pool was filled, the last leaves swept
into heaps to be bagged and carted.
Then Mr. and Mrs. Friedman argued.
She wanted more done. The men were nervous.
Cars might come along Kingview Road.
So far, not one had passed.

There was that house, at hilltop,
whose windows frowned down

on all their summers, a house
that just a dozen years back
had hosted a rally of sheeted rioters.

Once, so it was told, some thirty thousand Klansmen
poured into town to terrify the Catholics.
Catholics then, but now the Jews and Negroes.
You worried about groups of men
riding on the back of a pickup truck
up to no good on a Saturday night.

The moonless night blazed with stars.
Shapes human and not,
moved in and out of the headlamps
as the Golem swept, and scrubbed,
and swept again. At the end of it all,
the Golem returned to the edge of the wood.

All looked with relief
at the still-black windows
of the big white house on the hill.
No light had come on up there.
No one had seen us.

Then I was raised once more
to retrieve the undecipherable scroll
that I knew, but did not tell them,
read "Emet," the word for Truth.
The clay mouth was wider, deeper
than when the Golem was made,
wide enough for a small boy
to fall in and be devoured.
                        "Go on!"
the Rabbi chided me. "He cannot bite.
He has no teeth. Just find the paper."
I reached, back till my elbow was wet
with clay. He smelled now of chlorine
and year-old leaves. I found it.
My fingers closed around it.

My head went back. My eyes
gazed straight into the emerald
furnaces of the Golem's still-living orbs.


*iv*
And I saw everything —
A high-domed palace of giants,
packed to the walls with them,
legion of lumbering Golem shapes
impatient to be born
from a place of good deeds unbidden,
of help that could have, but never came —
the nullity of unworked magic
and failed alchemy.

I saw new kinds of geometry —
triangles unnamable
through which the news of past
and future calamities flies
like telegraphs, most sent
to wrong recipient, and read too late --
how triangles, upward and downward
formed openings, how spun they formed
vast polyhedrous entities
whose facets were the insides
of never-opened geodes,
arched around gateways
of onyx and adamantine —

Vectors of force and how
to form and shape them
from nothing but will,
nudged by the eye
in forehead's center
into a brooding shape
of inward angles
then up and out bat-winged
hurled down as a smiting force
upon the smiters —

Power I saw, but not compassion,
a dark, cold cavern
despite the light of whirling wish-forms
and the firefly storm of eyes
the color of emeralds.

*v*
I think I fainted.
The Rabbi, the Friedmans
stood in a circle around me.
A cold cloth was on my forehead.
"Thank God," said Mrs. Friedman,
"we don't have to call an ambulance."
The Rabbi leaned down
    and hissed in my ear:
"Did you see? Did you see?"

I dared not smile, despite
    the exultant knowledge
that flooded over me.
"I saw," I answered simply.
He paused, eyes shining.
"I saw ... everything."

He raised his hands in horror,
then waved two counter-circles
    above my head
as if to cut a cord above me.

I went back home. I added
the Hebrew-lettered paper
to my *Famous Monsters* scrapbook,
Golem marked off between
"Frankenstein" and "Mummies."
I had an ovoid sandstone
warm in the palm, I dubbed
"The Philosopher's Stone,"
thought it would help make
little Golems I'd shape one day.

The following week
     the Rabbi ignored me
as I carried ice and card-decks
to the women's tables.
The darting eyes of Mrs. Friedman
said *Don't you dare tell.*

I stood off in the pines to watch.
The women sunbathed and played at cards.
The shirt-sleeved men kept apart
as one by one they came to the Rabbi's table
and passed him envelopes, a stack
before him by the end of the afternoon.
They had done their part against Krushchev.

He watched them. He watched them watching
as one another's wives dived in
to the deep end of the swimming pool.
His back was to the women.
After one walk uphill to the clay bank —
just to be sure it had resumed its previous state,
I guessed — he went to his car. I waved.
I think he saw me. I think a slight nod
was his only thank-you. I was the clay
he could not put back from where it came.

Not to worry. I am still
not a Christian.

vi
Rabbi, The Golem said to tell you:

*A hammer is as nothing*
     *without a hand to wield it.*
*A hand is as nothing*
     *without a mind to guide it.*
*A mind is as nothing*
     *without the will to drive it*
*The will is as nothing*
     *without the gift of knowing*

*Knowing is as nothing*
  *without the love that burns*
*at the core of the never-dying stars:*
*love of what was, love of what is,*
  *love of what can be.*


   *(The Golem's message in Yiddish)*

   A hammar iz gornisht
   felndik a hant
   tsu vild es.

   A hant iz gornisht
   felndik a gayst
   tsu firn es.

   A meynung iz gornisht
   felndik di vilpauer
   tsu for es.

   Vilpauer iz gornischt
   felndik di talant
   fun visn.

   Veyst iz gornischt
   felndik di libe
   vos brent
   in di harts
   fun imortal shtern:

   libe aoyb vos iz geven,
   libe aoyb voz iz,
   libe aoyb vos kenen zeyn.

<53>

# CRACKERS AT MIDNIGHT

Midnight has passed. The kerosene lamp
is the only thing on in the kitchen.
I tip-toe out for our secret ritual.
"Hungry again?" my grandmother asks,
I nod. There wasn't much to eat
now that the garden had browned out
and snow came up to the porch-step.

In the tiny pool of yellow light
on the oilcoth-covered table,
she opens a stack of saltine crackers,
splits the wax paper wrapping
to a domino line of leaning squares,
salt-crackled and crisp. The dish
of butter was already waiting.
With one broad knife she spreads
the golden soft butter on one,
then two, then half a dozen.

Hunched over the cracker feast,
we nibble as quietly as mice.
In every room, the sleepers breathe.
We bite — one snorts — we chew —
another begins to snore — we swallow —
as someone moans and turns to one side.
They never hear us, and never will.

"One more?" my grandmother asks me,
broad butter knife in hand.
"Just one," I say. If I eat one,
she eats another. Somehow we always
find two at the bottom.

A cup of spring water to wash them down,
a good-night wave at the kitchen door,
and I creep back to bed. You never
go to bed hungry if a grandmother is there.

# NIGHT WALKER

Still in her nightgown,
    the wiry old woman,
    nearly a skeleton in satin,
    sleepwalked through lawns,
    onto a well-known path,
    passing her mother's grave,
barefoot between the Civil War cannons,
out the back gate,
then down the slope to the river.

Imagine her walk,
untouched by thorn and burr,
oblivious to gravel,
then over rail and tie
without a splinter,
then gravel again,
then down the steep bank
to the summoning waters!
(Silt, fish, and flotsam flow
from Youghiogheny to Gulf —
how far might she go?)

Cats she'd once fed
watched from the dark
of rhododendrons,
   but did not go to her.
I saw her, too,
   mute and astonished
as she passed the monument
where I recited *Ulalume* —

The cold chill current
did not awaken her,
lifted her up from her wading.
Weeds and crayfish
merged with her streaming hair.

She sank, her gown
a luminescent ribbon,
pulsing like a jellyfish,
for an instant, ageless —
Ophelia or water nymph,
Rhine Maiden, Lorelei —
sparked like an electric eel,
and then the water
was black on black.
Her life dissolved
in unseen bubbles.

Who beckoned her?
What star deluded her?
What long-dead lover
   called from the mud
   of the river bottom?

# ELDORADO

I searched the angry street
and the dismal forest gloom,
I spanned the globe, and yet
no one has shown me Eldorado!
Who, gaily bedight,
has seen the golden walls,
its ingot walks,
in the soft effuse
of a Mexican sunset?
Who, amid the mango groves
and phosphorescent parrots
shall tread the wayward avenues
of burnished gold,
beneath a golder moon?
Are they dead, those feathered, tawny men,
those speakers of Mayan tongues,
those carvers of
all-but-unreadable stones?
Who has closed the great earth
and silenced the horns
of Eldorado?
Who has been there and returned? —
madmen and dreamers!

One night on the shore of a lake,
(a Northern lake, no hint of summer!)
as I lay
in a bed of warm, expiring leaves
a low voice whispered:
*Silence is the road to Eldorado* . . .

Then, one December night
we walked, we two
(I thought you were the one foretold)
on an incredible avenue
of snow-filled trees
cupolas filled with myriad crystals,
the lake

a fractal-fractured spiderweb of ice
and there, in that unbroken loneliness of snows
in a stillness so still
we could hear the trees inhale,
we watched, touched finger to finger,
as on the frozen lake three spires arose
and out of the ice great glimmering stones
climbed up. The moon blushed. The breeze
caught its breath. It had always been there
and had only to be called
by the stillness of two not speaking,
falling into the abyss of dead irises
and conjunct heartbeat. *Eldorado!*

How long did it remain there,
where any passing stranger might
have stepped beyond its threshhold
into glory and untold riches?

Only so long as we said nothing
did it burn the backs of our eyes,
gilding our brains with memories.
And only so long as I never said
I loved you, was it as real as this,
as tangible as mirror glass, as cold
as frozen steel, and yet as barred from us
as though a dragon flamed up
between us and Eldorado.


2
Call it Eldorado,
city of dread truth and light, harbor of the mind,
city built out yet built by no one.
If I show you my Eldorado, make clear its walls
and towers from the fog, would you step into it?
Can it be real
while being all that you ever dreamt?
Is its wealth in ingot and bullion,
in dead weight a dead man may carry?

Or is it the city of Ideal Men,
whose treasure is that all who inhabit it
are inherently good, virtue's automatons,
soldiers valiant and incorruptible?

Can it be visible to you?
Could you address them
if you have killed your heroes?
If you are so unlike the graven greats
on the walls of Eldorado,
would you know them as brethren?
Would mothers, sisters, brides and daughters
of this proud Atlantis hail you,
or avert their eyes in loathing?

Shall not this city recede from us, then?
No matter how sharp the vision, each step
toward it takes us astray or backwards.
In silence we see it clear; in speech
it grows dim and cloaks itself in fog.
If I say nothing, my hand can almost reach
to the edge of one great turreted tower.
And yet, because I love you, I say
"There is nothing there, no city.
The sun on the ice makes fools of us.
Our eyes are not to be trusted. At home,
beside our fire, beneath the blankets
of an oblivious bed, is what is real.
My hand on neck-nape, on shoulder;
your hand as I raise it to palm-kiss;
these things are gold and silver."

Gone the city. Not one gold flake have I
to prove it ever existed. And just as gone
the ice-blind illusion of loving:
you no more knew me than you knew
a maple's groan in the frosted air.
I have no token of your having lived.

# NEW YEAR'S DAY

The meal is, shall we say,
   *monochromatic:*
in the cramped dining nook
with a hard-white beam
   of afternoon sun
chiaroscuro, bouncing off
white table-cloth, white china,
the white serving-platter
   of pale roast pork,
the pearly-white of mashed spuds,
chalky pork gravy,
off-color rancid butter,
bread — white, of course,
   no other, ever —
white paper napkins,
the pale complexions
of the right kind of people.

Stepfather presides
over a Swede Lutheran silence.
No one is permitted to speak,
save for *pass-this-pass-that*
and *thank-you.* The only sounds
are knife-scrapes and fork bites,
the shuffle of chairs
   against the splintered floor,
the stifled winter cough.
Mother says nothing; beer
   has done its work.
Stepfather has no use
   for the two stepsons,
book-reading idlers and spawn
of the man he hated and replaced.
Still, as long as the child-support
checks came every month,
he'd have to feed them.

Nothing has any flavor.
White salt, passed round,
and added liberally,
helps not so much as pepper,
lots of it, and water aplenty.
Food cooked in hatred
can only be *washed down*,
    not eaten.

Ignoring the shouted order
to "excuse himself."
the older boy gets up,
takes empty water-glass
to the kitchen sink,

and standing there,
he gazes into the sunlit nook,
at the hazed sunbeam
below the unlit chandelier,

from whose never-dusted
maze of dangling crystals,
*descended*

on pale white threads of silk
hundreds upon hundreds
of
tiny
white
baby
spiders

onto the white pork
the white bread
the white gravy
the white potatoes
the white tablecloth
the white paper napkins

onto the stern whiteness
of the Stepfather,
the passive Mother,
the little brother
gobbling away
at gravy-bread.

Does he tell them?
Or does he run outside
howling with laughter,
thanking the cosmos
for just desserts?

# THE OWL

*from The God's Eye: A Summer Diary*

We walk the forest in drizzling rain,
pretending not to mind it, every now
and then wiping water from hair and brow,
conscious of one's earth-and-grass clogged
boots getting heavier by the moment.
Ben strides ahead, proud and happy
to share the peace of his hundred acres,
Hannah beside him, helping to name and observe
the thousand species of shrubs and berries,
the untamed tangle of farmer's woodlot.
The soil is shallow, Ben tells me, so trees
grow only so high until inadequate roots
no longer withstand the leverage of wind —
and so the giants topple and die. And yet
we come upon that stately ash,
its trunk a hundred years or more across,
its leaves like knives or spears defying
the wind next time, the winters yet to come.
There is always one exception to a law.
Moving to field and orchard, Ben names
the sapling fruit trees, remarks how few
will grow in this stingy-summered North.
Here it is order — next to the female tree
with its bridal blossoms, placed at a kind
but respectful distance, a male companion.
Down there, in the chaos of tangled wood,
blueberries thrust through inverted tree trunks,
wild flowers wait for the inadvertent bee,
things grow because they must,
                              as if by accident.
In this new orchard, and the measured garden
from which, an unapprenticed sorceress,

Hannah can fill her bounteous table,
there is a balanced order. The sun,
defying the thermodynamics of entropy,
provides the energy, the man and woman
the order, the choices, the impetus.
                                                  We turn,
and crossing the knee-high grass of the field,
we are transfixed as a feathered shape
leaps down from a twisted shard of tree.
Amazed but curious, we circle it,
find a great owl with wings unfurled,
staring us down, holding a circle of ground
as a warning. No less surprised than we,
it turns its head in an impossible arc
to register the whole horizon of us.
We walk away. The curve of hill,
the sweep of grass, conceal us.

Later we sit, warmed by our red-bark tea,
and ask ourselves, "Was the owl hurt?
Was it protecting a nest? Why did it choose
to spread its wings and execute
that clumsy and alarming dance,
when it could have flown and vanished?"

I, too, dropped out of the sky to visit you.
I do not know why I came.
My hosts are not just farmers
but college folks,
the house has more books by far
than rakes or pitchforks.
Ben talks about his research
and the damn fools
who refuse to understand him;
how they broke their post-
retirement promises and took away
his lab, his tiny office space.

I talk about my poetry
    and the damn-fool publishers who won't —
    you know the rest.

After dinner,
I spread my wings and dance
    the halting dance of my poems.
He tries as hard to understand me
as I, his bioelectrochemistry.

(Later I'll get a letter from him
suggesting I do something more practical
with the brain the gods gave me — ha!
as though I had a choice!)

But for now,
night-bird and poet,
twine this rainy reunion
with our inexplicable presence,
knotting the thread of time
with an omen and a blessing.

# TABLEAUX FROM
# A PENNSYLVANIA VILLAGE

1
*Cloud Actors*
Spotlit to the last,
the thunderheads recede
southeast, in sunset red,
like hoary-headed thespians
unwilling to *exeunt*
without a proper flourish.

Inside the clouds,
the stubborn lightning
flashes, as if another act
of *Hamlet* or *Lear*
required its illumination.
The last of day
does not take curtain calls,
trailing the curtain of eventide
it rolls off the storm's advance
into the night's
dark amphitheater.
The lights go out.

2

*The Bats At Dusk, The Ducks Withdraw*
See them now, dart silhouette
in their new-bird pride!
The bats — presumptuous mice —
take wing, *upwards* on a twilit wind,
*downwards* into a gnat-rich dusk.

As ducks float south,
the backs of white mallards
turn like the final page
of a silk-lined novel,
flap shut in sun-gem's fall
from weeping willow tapestry.

From the bridge I eye flock's
    cooling retreat,
the "V" of their coming
an almost-"A" arrow departing
passive in downstream current,
each quack from on the water
answered by croak
from a somnolent frog.

Above the processional,
the celebrant fledermice,[1]
afloat on sonar-guided updraft,
feasting on bug-fest
    with open mouths,
squeak-flap-chitter their exultation,
beat on past dusk
    toward the stars.

---

[1] *Fledermice*. The bat in German is *Die Fledermaus*.

3

*War of the Lake Against Its Borders*
In war, old men give out the orders —
    the young men march out and die.
The already-dead in their Civil War,
World War One and Two plots, silent lie,
drum-taps and bugles and epaulets gone.
Nothing down there in the lakeside graveyard
but pine-box rot and the long slur of worms,
but up here, the ancient maples have made
against wind and water, a palisade,
gray warriors stiff-stern at the lake-edge.

They bend their grave green heads in counsel, brush
shagged samaras in a windy tumult,
send gossip-squirrel couriers to branch-
end, the golden leaflets propelling down,
leaf-pile wind-pushed advance to battlefield.
They argue tactics, instruct the saplings,
shudder in windy speeches, arthritic.
They are the proud maple-leaf generals.
The Lake is their ancient, blind nemesis.
A hundred years they have contained him.
Root-strong, they know they will one day surround
and absorb him, tame him to pond, to puddle.
to a mere widening of snow-filled creeks.

His Majesty the Lake must be content
to weave a plot for the millennium,
to gnaw on pebbles ignominious,
to swell with the creek-and-rainfall tribute,
smug at the man-made dam that deepened him.
He dreams of expanded borders, does naught
but lap his decadent breakers, weak-wan
against sand and silt of the pebbled shore,
hunched in the kettle the glaciers carved him.
He frightens no one, looks to mystic clouds
for auguries, sleeps in the afternoons,
interrogates the fishes and flotsam,
attempts to read news from the incoming Braille
of pelting rain drops (all reassuring),
traces lake's ice cracks in dead of winter
but fails to detect the coded messages.
No one betrays the tree-army's secrets.

Now it is spring. The officers conspire,
draw from sun-dew a seedling explosion.
They raise up a line of green colossi:
rusty, bellicose day lily dragons
issue their challenge to cowardly waves.
Others are drafted, too: spies creep
toward the water in a bed of moss.
Fern leaves unfurl their flagrant green pennants.
Foot soldier fungi pop up red-capped, spores
ready to replenish their short-lived selves.
Roots furrow underground, touch hands and hold.

Lake's King has weapons, too: one night a fog
clouds up the foe's senses in fairy mist.
Then comes the rain — an equinoctial storm —
A night of cold downpour — a deluged day —
a night more of of starless, moonless cloudburst.
Waves batter-ram the tree-line barricades.
Muscles renewed and tendons vivified,
he roars like an ocean, spews tidal spray.

The border army breaks, then mends, then holds.
Where roots had lost the soil to cling to,
a tree falls willingly to barricade
with leaf and limb and sundered trunk.
Where water attempts to break the land,
elsewhere, a rope-tough vine, a wild-rose thorn,
a dead-tree pike-shaft punctures him. Roots hold.
Howling and humbled the Lake-King retreats.
His waves recede to a mirror stillness.

At sun-up, the silver orb of Venus
looks down and sees her own slender crescent;
bird echoes bird-arc in parallel flight;
each cloud regards his symmetric brother.
The tangled flora begins to heal itself.
Who won the war? Look at the lake edge now,
see that parade-line stiff and pluming there,
as day lilies burn gold against the light!

*4*
*Stormy Day in Spring*
No one goes out on these cloudy days.
The forest is empty. A willow tree
burns in first green, vibrant
against a red-gray skillet of clouds.
Was green ever greener than this?
This is the secret hue of spring,
saved for the rainy-day elite!

The civilized ones! They are all indoors
with damp umbrellas, their soggy shoes drying,
while I stand here on the stream bed,
alone as though their world had ended.
I look at the backs of houses: no one
comes down to the water-edge
to exult with me in willow-rapture.

Keep your clapboards and chimneys!
Give me this brooding, north-born sky,
the ardent chill of this windy noon —
give me a little sun — a beam or two
to slice the scudding rain clouds,
splash rainbows on the canopy
of gray and brown and emerald.

Give me this — there is nothing sweeter
than this encompassing embrace!
To be alive, alone
amid the willows and the indifferent rain,
to be at the apex of consciousness —
to feel the very pulse of life evolving —
green! green and alive upon the world!

# LETHE

Deliver the fruit of the garden of Lethe!
The white horse of sleep is at home in his stable,
mane twined with coca and hemp leaves,
neck wreathed in poppies, his breath a cloud
of Hypnos' hashish. He feeds on hay,
mixed rich with ergot and mushrooms.

The white horse of sleep goes forth,
draws a black coach through city streets,
pauses in alleyways,
lingers at school-yards.
A dark hand hurls cigarettes,
bags and vials, syringes and pipes,
toys scattered with whispered promises
of power and wealth and instant joy.
Boys fight for the poisoned apples.

Mothers shake fists from fire escapes
as the white horse passes.
On curbs, on broken bench,
in frame of rotted door,
the sleepers have fallen.
Others fan out to sell their treasures.
There is never enough.
Someone must always pay —
even here where no one has money —
or someone must die.

Some days the white horse pulls
a great stone Juggernaut.
The children run to greet it,
and one by one are pulled beneath.
Iron wheels burr
with shattered bones,
grindstone steam roller
makes lithography of skin,
cheekbones and brows,
limb and arm and ribcage

spread out like a map,
dreamers' lives snuffed
into a red-brown inkblot.

The mothers' sons
are crimson smears on the sidewalk.
Mica glints mockingly
as blood dries to flaking rust.
Silence, then choked weeping,
and then the sound of the Juggernaut
rumble-crush rolling
on distant streets, the muted screams
diminuendo to deathly quiet.

Uptown, at the fashionable clubs,
no horse-drawn carriage comes.
Instead, the white stretch limos
arrive and depart,
arrive and depart.
A movie star falls to the pavement,
dead of an overdose
at twenty-two.
Inside, the revelers
compare the merits
of various white powders.
No Juggernaut comes for them:
the white limo doubles
as a hearse when necessary.

They are politically correct,
    vegetarian, even.
They are supporting
    the produce
of the endangered rain forest.
Nothing could possibly hurt them.

# MOTHERHOOD

Trailer park slattern, blonde,
    holds close two flax-haired children.
"We need another genocide,"
    she says to the camera,
more opioid mama than Viking
    shield maiden.
"You know that means killing?"
    the reporter asks.
She nods. "I know. We need
    to have another genocide." —
"You know that means killing women,
    and all their children with them?" —
Her eyes drop, then raise. "I know that." —
    "So why do we need another genocide?" —
"Them!" she shouts, pointing at progeny,
    "So my children will have a chance."
Husband, off camera: "That's my woman.
    Ain't she something?"

# WARTIME FRAGMENT

*Bellum/bella*
  *ante*
  *inter*
  *post*

was this a just war, an old men's war?
a war of merchants who wanted their weapons used,
so that the great treasures of two kingdoms passed
o, into *their* hands, Vulcan's malevolent sons?

O the why and wherefore of war, what reckoning
your heirs will make of it, beside a ruined tomb!

# NERO AND THE FLAMINGO

He is the Emperor
of the known universe:
of Rome, that is,
and of every place
worth having.

The gods are best pleased
by ever-more-exotic
sacrifices.
No lowly chickens here
in Rome whose temples
all but outstrip Olympus.
Give up the cattle to Jove,
and to that upstart Mithra;
meek lambs and smelly rams
fit only for Judaean
hecatombs. No,
only the best for Nero,
the whole menagerie
if need be, to assure
his eventual,
glorious godhood.

Today he picks a stately
bird, a solitary feeder
that keeps to its own corner
in a flush of pink feathers.
Hook-nose wary,
it is a half-arm taller
than his Centurions.
He waits at the altar.
It is all legs and beak,
scratches and snaps at the priests
as they hold it down.

Nero approaches
with the drawn blade,
intones the prayer,
slashes the place
where gangly neck
and pink body converge.

The head comes off.
The body leaps up
and out of the priest-hold,
spurts blood
all over Nero's toga.
No one moves; no one utters
a syllable; all of Rome's heart
skips a beat. Crowds part
as the headless horror
runs out and down the temple steps,
across the plaza, a blood-Aetna
bespattering the paving stones.
Crowds part for its passing
until it reaches the Tiber
and plunges in.

The Emperor stands,
the knife in hand,
his toga bloodied, ruined.
The priests avert their eyes.
Centurions watch
as less-than-divine hands
wipe blood on white linen;
they look at one another
and with a not-quite smile,
the same thought occurs
to each of them.

# DREAMERS

The hand extended to an innocent child,
the hand snapped back; the slap
back-handed, the raised club,
the road-side stop, the knock
three times at the midnight door.
Dark-celled without a lawyer,
then bused to a border, and over it.
One hand, with a pen-stroke
(small fingers tweeting), eight
hundred thousand eye-blink exiles.
What list are you on, reader,
and when does your time come?

# WHO CAN BE A POET ALL OF THE TIME?

Who can be a poet all of the time?
The sons of rich fathers,
    remittance men —
spinster heiresses with hyacinth hair,
    filling long sheets with
        delicate verse —
the wrinkled don retired at last
    to his monument of sonnets —
the very young — the truly mad —
    the Muse-possessed
(not just visited, *inhabited*
    by the poem-urge) —

But for the rest of us,
    being a poet
is at best an illusion,
    at worst a vice.
A thing of glory, certainly.
    Honor or profit?
        not in this age!

Against those *professionals*,
we migrant poets must distill
    into a hundred poems,
the brandy of *their* thousands,
lift up our frail mimosa leaves
beneath *their* sky-
    consuming oaks.

*They* are at it, day and night.
The mail truck groans
with their outgoing manuscripts.
They teach this stuff.
Honest to God, they are paid to do it!
They sniff at one
    another's résumés.

Their blurbs adorn
    each other's jackets.
They are weighed down with medals
they give to one another with wink and nod.
They eat the flesh of rivals,
trample their peers,
for something called "tenure."

The rest of us must steal these hours,
scrawl debtors' ink
    on dime-store paper,
consort with the Muse
    as though adulterous,
secret as those frenzies
in the alleys of Sodom
between the angels
    and the damned.

In the anvil world we live in
we are impractical, slothful,
lounging for adjectives
when we should be "working,"
shouting our newfound lines
against the surf,
    to the dead in graveyards,
to the astonished grackles
    on our window ledge —

while *they*
    winter in Cancun,
laze at the MacDowell colony,
turn slowly drunkard
and sad as their students
no longer sleep with them —

for us, it is
    absolutely useless, this
    rootless, anti-
        Puritan ethic obsession —

Except that for these moments,
    freely given,
    we would nothing trade,
knowing that those who follow us
would forfeit fortunes, too,
    for such a poetic seizure,
would trade a life of ease,
    for hard-wrought poems
that tread the space
    between the stars.

# SWAN LAKE VARIATIONS

*1*
Turns out there are twelve
alternative endings.
No one will leave *Swan Lake*
alone in its sound-world,
its gloom trajectory.

The cast: Prince Siegfried:
you know the type.
Irresolute, with the kind
of mother too well renowned:
"Just pick one. Any one.
I'll have you married, young man."
Odette, who was once a woman,
now doomed to swanhood
in a white tutu.
Rothbart the sorcerer,
in dusty owl-gear, his gig
to turn women to waterfowl.
His daughter, Odille,
black swan seducer.

How many endings
with climactic storm,
forest confusion,
deaths and drownings?

The Prince beats Rothbart
and tears a wing off,
stealing his swan-girl away.
She'll be a human bride
by the time they get to Mother.

Or, the Prince shoots Rothbart
with his magic crossbow.
Odette forgives him
for cheating with Odille
just hours before.
It's a comedy of manners.

Or, sometimes Odette *does* drown
(hard work for a water-bird),
and Siegfried joins her.
Each clambers up in turn
to precipice and leaps.

Or, Soviets want a happy ending,
and get one, a fairy tale
to undo the melancholy
of too-long winters.
Love defies magic; Rothbart
just sinks to lake-mud —
*Bozhe moi*, let him have the girl.

Or, Nureyev chooses the death-leap.
Rothbart and the swan-bride
soar heavenward, the gay prince
relieved in death to be spared
a tutu wedding night.

And, in New York, two suicides
break Rothbart's spell.
The lovers ascend
in Wagner apotheosis.

Or, Odette is condemned
to be just a swan,
a haggard water-fowl.
The disillusioned prince
stands there and sulks.
Maybe they'd roast her
for the wedding feast.

Or, the Prince and Rothbart wrestle.
In their exhausting struggles,
both drown. Odette remains,
the nineteenth swan, odd-out
in every choreography.

Or, the eighteen swans
peck Rothbart to death.
Owl-feathers and bones
sink to the lake's bottom.
Odette and Siegfried
take bows and marry.

Or, a promise being a promise,
Siegfried marries Odile,
the bad swan, becomes
the sorcerer's son-in-law.
Odette droops wings,
Swan Cinderella.


2
*Swan Lake in Pittsburgh*
Disheartened by happy ending
tacked on to Tchaikovsky's
gloom-ridden ballet —
the drowned white swan Odette,
and the drowned Prince Siegfried
seen floating past, as good as new
on Lohengrin's swan-raft —

*Really?* Amid lamenting coda,
piled high with tragedy,
this Disney charade
so that little girls in tutus
sitting in the balcony
don't go home crying?

<85>

Odette's body, swollen,
entangled in algae,
washed up on shore
three days ago.

As for the Prince,
he was found, a "floater"
beneath the Sixth Street Bridge.
Eels came from his mouth
when they hooked
the bloated corpse.
The grieving Queen
was inconsolable.

Rothbart, that bloated owl,
swan-pimp,
still lords it
with the eighteen virgins
he lured away to suicide
(three rivers here, and lots
of unhappy girls!).
Each night they rise
and dance their cygnette
sarabande, with a harp,
a violin and a cello.
Other young men
they will lure to drowning.
That filthy owl,
man-hating sorcerer,
knows only this game
and never loses.

# LINES OVERHEARD
## AT THE RUSSIAN TEAROOM

Ludmilla's got herself a husband.
It doesn't matter that you're stupid
if you can dance *en pointe*.

The tables are so close here:
There's Donald Trump,
only one hand visible.
Two tables down, that model
from all the magazines.
That dowager between
with that look on her face?
The poor man can't count.

*Ya piu nad razorenni dom.*
*(I drink to our ruined house).*
Why did we have to build it
in Florida?

It was, of course,
a Jewish conspiracy.

There is no evidence.
Besides, we already have
the green cards for everyone.

So we played. We knew the music.
He stood there waving his stick.
He was two beats behind us
and never knew the difference.

No one finds the bodies.
No one. They say he keeps
the eyeballs. He pickles them.

I have a friend at Coney Island.
For you, he will fix everything.

Ignore the news, Sergei.
Everything goes
the way we planned it.

How many people here
would stop dead-track
if I said "Moose and Squirrel?"

# VARIATIONS ON THE IBIS

*1*
Artists are people to whom coincidence
adheres, filings to their magnet consciousness.
My painter friend Riva points out
a small montage, a hulking splotch
with linked chains and a few squiggles.
"It won some prizes," she tells me,
"But as for what it means —" she shrugs.
My eyes reel into its story-window:
I see Prometheus chained, a Grand Inquisitor
in purple robes, and there, the white wings
of the gloating Zeus-eagle. "I can write this,"
I tell her. "Take it," she said.

Another time she shows me an etching,
a crinolin'd ghost shape a-dance
before a barren landscape. It sits
the bottom-most discard in a bottom drawer.
"That is the Empress Carlota!" I cry,
"And that is Queretaro where Maximilian died."
So off I went and wrote a play.

On a graveyard walk she stops, leans down
and picks up a squashed shard, some scrap
of one car's fender run over by another.
"I'll make something of this," she told me.
I carry it home in my bag, then place
it absent-mindedly on dresser-top.
Months later, she visits and spies it,
atop a wood frame. I pick it up
to hand it back to her. Our eyes dance
upon the seeming-shapeless object,
and then to what's inside my glass-framed box:
the Indonesian fruit-bat I nicknamed "Claudius."
The shape of the found object precisely fills
the silhouette of the preserved fruit bat.
We smile. This is how the universe works us.

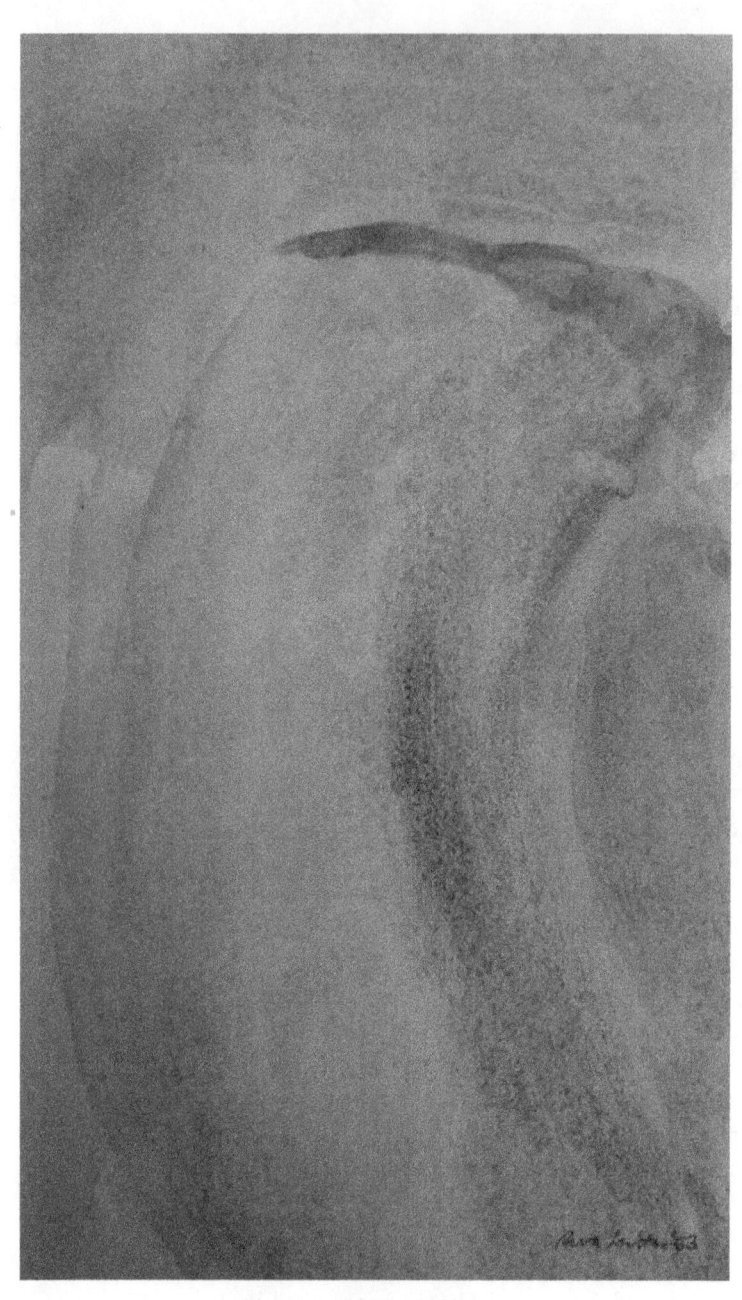

Small wonder, then, that I am reading Egypt,
the lore of Thoth and Hermes, his totem
animals the Lower Kingdom's lordly ibis,
the Upper Kingdom's wise baboon,
when tea with Riva reveals a water color
mystery, a scimitar shape emerging
from a blue-gray mist, a river fog,
a scythe, perhaps, with a hand to wield it.
"No!" I said. "It is upside-down."
And there, in lordly solitude,
stood the Egyptian ibis. I have it still.
Riva is gone, her mind first, and then her body,
the *ka* and the *ba* on out-of-kilter journey
across to the Land of Reeds in the West.
So now the ibis painting is in its place
at my compound shrine of Hermes-Thoth:
the ibis with kneeling scribe before it,
the ibis-headed god himself in sculpture;
the sacred baboon, his upper-Nile double;
the head of Hermes; two small pyramids,
a hippo, and *The Book of Coming Forth by Day*.

2
I asked a Greek who'd been to Egypt,
an Alexandrian admittedly, about the ibis.
"Don't mention ibises! Those filthy birds,
worse than the legendary Harpies, be sure.
Not just the stately water-strider
you see in those temple scrolls — no!
Packs of them in every garbage heap,
fish-trash and butcher dumping place,
they scarf what jackals would scorn to swallow.
They eat anything! They gorge themselves
until their innards can take no more —
guts forty yards long, I can assure you —
until they're fat as pampered geese.
The ibis knows no repose from gluttony:
stuffed full, it goes off to the water.
Then, cheeks and bill blown up,
it gives itself a water enema.

The stench amid the reeds
is not to be believed.
No one will eat an ibis, I tell you,
and fishermen at night have seen them
beak to belly in oral copulation.
(You can look it up in Strabo, too!
I'm not making this up.)
Now what this says about the priests of Thoth,
those ibis-headed ministers
and their mystery rites,
is best left to the imagination.
Would you eat at table with a man
who had such habits? One cup
his lips had touched could fell a village.
I'm not one to leap to conclusions,
but I prefer my gods sunny, Greek, and clean."

## THE COMPANY OF AN EAGLE

I have a date
with my eagle lover —
bird-killing bird,
rabbit hunter,
assassin of squirrels,
sneak-thief of cub and kitten.
His prominence
(one- or two-headed)
on flags and coins,
seals and warplanes
must have enthralled me.
And of course he might,
just might be Zeus in disguise.
I cleared my calendar,
cleaned house,
turned balcony
into a landing pad/eyrie.
Maybe my kind enjoy
being swooped down upon.

The phone will not ring.
The door chime
hoards expectant silences.
Nothing will precede him
except an updraft
and the sound of wingbeats.

Wingbeats, yes. The dull
thud of contact, then
something rolls
into my living room,
the outspread wings and talons
guiding it.

That predator egg he brought
sits on the couch
between us,
and if it hatches,
what then of dinner and wine
and candlelight?

Will the eaglet choke down
my proffered feast,
preening his downy feathers
and asking for more?

When our *entre nous*
becomes a raptor nursery,
shall our tryst be forgotten?
Will his nestling stay, too,
curled in my laundry hamper?
Isn't there a *Mrs.* Eagle
to take charge here?
Dare I tip-toe out and back
from the bathroom
without the admonishing screech
of its never-abating hunger?

If the egg is still,
will he remain then
to hear my poems,
to loan me his wingspan,
his shadow, his mute
but overarching company?

Or is it just about *him*?
"Look, I have made an egg!"
He never said there was a she-eagle,
or that he's a single dad-in-waiting.
It may not hatch at all.
What if it's dead?
What if it's only good
for making an omelet?

I could have chosen wolf,
    or lion, sky-hawk or tiger
    as my companion.
But here we sit, the eagle,
    the egg and I,
the embarrassed silence,
the shudder of wing-shrug,
the raptor eye fixed on me.

There is nothing else to do.

Slowly, I begin to undress.

# FRONTIER

Frontier is defined
as that which beyond
which is irrevocable danger:

eternal dusk
beyond the clearing of forest,
the padding wolf,
the lurking Savage/

a book of white pages
where no pen has gone,
dune after dune
unstained by ink/

the distance between us:
our hands have not yet touched
and hesitate as though
some killing amperage
lurked in opposing poles/

the terror of first buttons,
of touching turned explorer,
of the point beyond play
where fiercer passions lie/

frontier at last is seen
as where you cannot go forward
without becoming citizen
of my dark kingdom,

and where I cannot
return without some victory —
a champagn'd kiss,
a falling together,
a storm-lit moment
of sky-impaling joy.

Or is it our doom to stand,
each at our wall,
because you wait for some divinity
to raise you up to lofty love?

And so it is,
that those I loved best,
I never touched at all.

# THWARTED

Among the ways I have tried to express it
was the arbor of roses over your door
constructed at night by carpenters,
tip-toed in raccoon quietude,
pounding felt-covered hammers and oiled nails --
the roses you snubbed to an icy death
that snowy morning you never looked up,
or back, suitcased to cab for that
solitary European vacation
I helped you plan /

Among the ways
were the moonlit serenatas with mandolins
that elbowed each other behind your fence.
The tenor who labored my verses, your name
he said had too many consonants, the high C
half-voice for the paltry fee I offered.
Yes, the same players who fell from the willows
attempting to get my poems heard
over the tomcat rhapsody
and the din of your air conditioner /

Among the ways
were the commonplace words, veiled in a blush
that punctuated our seldom discourse. Not even
"Hello" could be dropped from the tongue single-edged.
Yes, the same words, like "dinner" and "alone" —
("Just us?" "Yes, the two of us." "Get back to you.") —
that registered blank in your eyes.
the silent phone, the cobwebbed mailbox
say all that need be said /

Among the ways
are those men left over from Fu Manchu
who follow your other admirers about
like dacoits, eyeing the alleys and parapets
for places to make their kill and escape.
Strange how your exes are turning up

dead, or missing/presumed, or reportedly
away with their new *inamorati*.
I never planned to spend so much
of my inheritance on hit men /

Among the ways
are the midnight oaths and promises
I make to dubious monarchs of love,
half-seen in the smog of my sulfurous hearth,
as I barter to Eros in Pluto's coinage
a year of my life, for a night of yours.
The incense clears, the brimstone pall
clears out to dawn-light, the mowers
start up at the edge of the graveyard,
and no, you are not there;
you are never there, nor will you be.
Cruel bargain, I am a year more old,
and you, a year younger. The gulf
already great between us, becomes a rift,
a continental shelf, extinction crater /

Be gone, be gone. I am done with this.

# PLEASE, NO

Two words, and almost always
unspoken,   *please, no*
a telepathic, eye-blink imperative

Choosing a side door
I've never seen before
I am revolving out
the Met Museum foyer
as Jackie Onassis,
head bowed, spins in
making her discreet entrance.
I do a double take.
Her great white eyes implore
*Please, no.*
My head dips down,
assenting. Her eyes
beam *Thank you.*
Her secret was safe with me.

On a New England street
I see a former loft-mate,
an art school graduate
I had coached toward
his first ad agency job.
I start to call his name,
then see his sunken cheeks,
the skeleton walk, the way
he leans against his friend.
He sees me. *Please, no.*
his deep-sunk eyes implore.
I turned away. Kenny
was dead a few months later.
His family erased him,
his epitaph an oak blast
wind, whispering
*Please, no.*

# WOOING

*adapted from Martial, I.x*

So, have you heard of Maronilla's wooing?
Gemellus is desperate,
and from a purse so small as his,
the presents he sends her, astonish.
We're taking bets on when the rites
will make him *Mister* Maronilla. But why?
Has she a young girl's charms to offer?
Not a chance — the hags of the town
use her as a model. What's this about,
you ask? Lean close as I whisper it:
she is rich, and she's tubercular.

# THE LOVED DEAD

*1*
Another year,
the sun resembles itself
but does not fool the trees
who shun its cool imposture.
Buds open reluctantly,
their slanted eyes askew
with annual doubts.
It is never the same,
each lap of light a ghost
of former springs, each ray
a waning monument
from where a darkling star
gluts space
with ever-diminishing mass.
The year we met,
is the immemorial year, the year
that cannot be repeated.

What world is this,
in which you do not wake,
and sleep, and call me?
The universe forgets itself —
the idiot sun implodes
into a fathomless mouth,
both feaster and food
adjourning to nothingness
at the event horizon.

The earth spins blindly on.
First, love can die.
And then the loved
    becomes the loved dead.
What if, in world-wipe,
you never existed?

*2*
I swear, I have not lost you.
Your disassembled eyes
rode in another's skull today.
I saw them — there was no blue
akin to your lapis irises.
Your disconnected arm
hooked onto mine at dusk.
(I walked alone, and blushed
at how and where
the hand-touch held me.)
Tonight before I slept
your mouth surprised me.
(The room was empty.)

It is better this way —
each bit of you a ghost
returning on an X-ray wind.
Each day some icy shard of you
drops off some glacial height
onto an unsuspecting face,
as though the gods that made you,
singular, keep trying
to make another.

The universe deceives itself.
One thing may be like another;
one thing is *not* the other.
Though ardent spring explodes
upon the feathered fields,
it is a new spring, slate clean.
The past — if there is a past —
is amnesia'd in wormhole transit
to the fiercely-blazing present.

I wait in solitude. If ghosts
could ever present themselves,
they'd rage because they could
    not say their names.
If phantom faces *seem* to be yours,
I love them for the lie they speak,
    of being you.

# NECROPOLIS

In park walk some years ago,
I came upon your ancestor's statue,
a Polish emigré who served
with General Washington.
He had your face. The bronze
had weathered little. I stood,
and stood, and could not stop looking.
Not acid rain, nor pigeon insult
had weathered it. I had you yet,
and yet had nothing. A few things
we touched in common, a bowl,
a red-glass pitcher whose breaking
I dreaded to think of. Not one photo.
Who is alive who ever
    saw us together?
What proof but memory,
    a weave of cell and synapse?

In the hard light
of this winter afternoon,
I am cheerful in graveyard
until I see the name
of one of your countrymen.
Sun sulks behind a sudden cloud
and I reel backwards, stumble-stop.
One day I thought that such as you
and I would live-walk the lanes
of all the earth's graveyards,
our laughter a leaf-pile
against the too-short days.

What now? Amid these tombs and columns,
sphinxes and obelisks, what is there left
but never-ending mourning?

What is there left
except to live on out
our ever-precious moments
in solitary tread, alone,
in their honor, and in their names?

The loved dead
who never come again
except in shards and glances,
moment of shuddering grief
and the remembering smile,

by what of you, and why,
am I haunted?

# POETS IN A CHELSEA BROWNSTONE

Hostess. I remember her hunched shadow
   on the frosted glass
   of the sliding French door,
as we poets read,

and how the door slid silently,
   just ever so much,
enough for the thin arm
   and age-knobbed wrist
to enter, to place
   on the refreshment table,
without one ice-clink sound,
the sweating-cool pitcher
   of lemonade.

Most of the eager poets
   assembled here,
tracked who-knows-what
   on her parquet floor,
shuffled their papers and notebooks,
awaited their turn to read,
yet did not know her name.

The elegant brownstone
   they came to weekly
   was just a place,
one among many
in *The Village Voice* listings,
   places that tolerate
the disheveled artists,
word-crazed, impractical,
the ones who will never
   earn a penny.

As I read in my turn,
   she listened there
behind the veil of glass,
a listening that leaned

on every consonant I uttered,
a keen pre-echo
    to every vowel.
Oh, she heard us.

We did not know her name,
or how the upstairs rooms lodged
a succession of broken souls,
her "causes,"
knew not that we'd been adopted, too.

One day, with a friend, I saw her,
emerging from the brownstone,
sun-walking Ninth Avenue,
behind some tugging hound
misfortune had doubtless thrust
    upon her charity.
The warm day reddened
    her parlor-pale face.

My friend tells me,
    "That's Mrs. Tanner, you know.
    That's *Auntie Mame!*"

# CHAUCER'S PROLOGUE TO THE PARLIAMENT OF FOWLES

*(A loosely metrical, free-verse adaptation, with slight explications of Cicero's Dream of Scipio.) This is in the form of a poetic improvisation, made without reference to any other modern English version and using only the glossary and notes for The Riverside Chaucer, Cicero's "Dream of Scipio," and the personal assistance of Hermes, the god of sudden inspiration.)*

Not years enough, in life so short,
to learn a craft so long, Ars longa, vita brevis
whose effort's hard, whose winning hurts,
whose painful joys slides snakily off —
by all this I mean Love, whose working
wonderful astonishes my senses,
so painful indeed, that when I think on it,
I know not whether I float, or fall.

    1 The Lyf so short, the craft so long to Lerne,
    2 Th'assay so hard, so sharp the conquerynge,
    3 The dredful joye, alwey that slit so yerne,
    4 Al this mene I by love, that my felynge
    5 Astonyeth with his wonderful werkynge
    6 So sore iwis, that whan I on him thinke,
    7 Nat wot I wel wher that I flete or synke.

Though practice of Love have I no knowledge,
nor of how well He pays his followers,
well have I read of his ways in books,
of both his miracles, and his cruelty.
There read I well, he will be Lord and master;
I dare not say how painful his strokes,
But "God give me such a Lord!" Ah, say no more!

   8 For at be that I knowe nat love in dede,
   9 Ne wot how that he quiteth folk hir hyre,
10 Yit happeth me ful ofte in bokes reede
11 Of his myralles, and his crewe yre.
12 Ther rede I wel he wol be lord and syre,
13 I dar not seyn, his strokes been so sore,
14 But "God save swich a lord!" — I can na moore.

What use is Love? a moment's friction or
a whole life's education? —
I read so many books, as I did say —
and why at all am I essaying this?
because just now I happened to behold a book,
a certain ancient text in antique tongues,
and there I sought to learn a Certain Thing,
so eager for it I read the whole day long.

15 Of usage, what for luste what for lore,
16 On bokes rede I ofte, as I yow tolde.
17 But wherfor that I speke al this? Not yore
18 Agon, hit happed me for to beholde
19 Upon a bok, was write with lettres olde,
20 And therupon, a certeyn thing to lerne,
21 The longe day ful faste I redde and yerne.

For out of old fields, as old wives say,
Comes the new corn from year to year,
Just so do old books, seen with new eyes
yield all that is new, that we call Science.
But now to get down to my business here:
reading that one book gave me such delight,
that all that day my own small soul seemed lost.

    22 For out of olde feldes, as men seyth,
    23 Cometh al this newe corn from yer to yere;
    24 And out of olde bokes, in good feyth,
    25 Cometh al this newe science that men lere.
    26 But now to purpos as of this matere:
    27 To rede forth hit gan me so delite,
    28 That al the day me thoughte but a lyte.

This book of which I make such mention —
I'll tell you how its title reads. It is:
The Dream of Scipio, as told by Cicero
(yes, Marcus Tullius, our old Roman friend!)
In only seven chapters, Heaven to Hell,
and Earth, and all the souls that dwell therein,
are all encompassed, and I mean
as quickly as I can, to share the gist.

    29 This bok of which I make of mencioun
    30 Entitled was al ther, as I shal telle,
    31 "Tullius of the Drem of Scipioun."
    32 Chapitres sevene hit hadde, of hevene and helle
    33 And erthe, and soules that therinne dwelle,
    34 Of whiche, as shortly as I can hit trete,
    35 Of his sentence I wol yow seyn the greete.

First off it says, when Scipio arrived
in Africa, to meet Massinissa, that King
of Numidia embraced him in joy –
they talked of his great forebear till the sun did fade.
Then in his sleep his ancestor appeared,
great Scipio Africanus, Carthage's conqueror!

>　36 Fyrst telleth hit, whan Scipion was come
>　37 In Affrike, how he meteth Massynisse,
>　38 That him for joie in armes hath inome.
>　39 Thanne telleth [it] here speche and al the blysse
>　40 That was betwix hem til the day gan mysse,
>　41 And how his auncestre, Affrycan so deere,
>　42 Gan in his slepe that nyght to hym apere.

The book relates, how from a starry place
the ancient Roman showed him Carthage
[the city he pillaged and sowed with salt],
forewarned him of his own ill providence,
and told him that any man, learned or ignorant,
that loved the common good, with virtue's ways —
that man shall go to a blissful resting place,
where joy without end awaits him.

>　43 Than telleth it that, from a sterry place,
>　44 How Affrycan hath hym Cartage shewed,
>　45 And warnede him beforn of al his grace,
>　46 And seyde hym, what man, lered other lewed,
>　47 That lovede commune profyt, wel ithewed,
>　48 He shulde into a blysful place wende,
>　49 There as joye is that last withouten ende.

And then he asked, if folk that here be dead
have life and dwelling in some other place,
and Africanus answered him, "Yes, doubt it not!"
and that the present life we live, whatever
way we go, is in itself a kind of death,
and that the righteous folk shal Heavenward wend;
and here, he showed the Galaxy

> 50 Thanne axede he, if folk that here been dede
> 51 Han lyf and dwellynge in another place.
> 52 And Affrican seyde, "Ye, withoute drede,"
> 53 And that oure present worldes lyves space
> 54 Nis but a maner deth, what wey we trace,
> 55 And rightful folk shul gon, after they dye,
> 56 To hevene; and shewed him the Galaxye.

And way below it, the little earth our home,
so tiny compared to the vastness of things.
Later, the ghost showed Scipio nine spheres.
from which he heard the harmonies and notes
that come by nature from thrice times three —
the wellspring of all music and melody,
the basis of all our harmony!

> 57 Than shewed he him the lytel erthe, that here is,
> 58 At regard of the hevenes quantite;
> 59 And after shewede he hym the nyne speres,
> 60 And after that the melodye herde he
> 61 That cometh of thilke speres thryes thre,
> 62 That welle is of musik and melodye
> 63 In this world here, and cause of armonye.

Then Africanus bade him: if the world is a mote,
deceptive and full of bad fortune,
to take no delight in this lower world.
Then he revealed to him, that ages hence
all the great stars will spin back home
from where they started, and all that man
has done in this world shall be forgotten.

    64 Than bad he hym, syn erthe was so lyte,
    65 And dissevable and ful of harde grace,
    66 That he ne shulde him in the world delyte.
    67 Than tolde he hym, in certeyn yeres space
    68 That every sterre shulde come into his place
    69 Ther it was first; and al shulde out of mynde
    70 That in this world is don of al mankinde.

Then he prayed Scipio to tell him
how he might himself arrive at Heaven's bliss
and the ghost said, "Know thyself first immortal,
then look to your work and direct yourself
to the common good — you cannot miss
your chance to come swiftly to that place
where clear souls live in eternal bliss.

    71 Thanne preyede hym Scipion to telle hym al
    72 The wey to come into that hevene blisse;
    73 And he seyde, "Know thyself first immortal,
    74 And loke ay besily thow werche and wysse
    75 To commune profit, and thow shalt not mysse
    76 To comen swiftly to that place deere,
    77 That ful of blysse is and of soules cleere.

"But breakers of the law, if truth be told,
and lecherous folk, once they are dead,
shall whirl about the earth in pain,
age upon, fearful age, and then at last
they shall be forgiven of their wicked deeds,
and they shall come into that blissful place,
where all who come to God receive his grace."

    78 But brekers of the lawe, soth to seyne,
    79 And likerous folk, after that they ben dede,
    80 Shul whirle aboute th'erthe always in peyne,
    81 Til many a world be passed, out of drede,
    8i And than, foryeven al hir wikked dede,
    83 Than shul they come unto that blysful place,
    84 To which to comen God the sende his grace!"—

The day had fallen, and gave way to night,
which robs all beasts of their business.
Men too — it was too dark to read —
and so, undressed for bed, I went —
my thoughts filled up with a heavy burden,
for I had a Certain Thing that I did not want,
and I did not have a Certain Thing I wished for.

    85 The day gan faylen, and the derke nyght,
    86 That reveth bestes from her besynesse,
    87 Berafte me my bok for lak of lyght,
    88 And to my bed I gan me for to dresse,
    89 Fulfyld of thought and busy hevynesse;
    90 For bothe I hadde thyng which that I nolde,
    91 And ek I ne hadde that thyng that I wolde.

But finally my spirit, at the last,
so weary from my labor of the day,
took rest and put me fast asleep,
and in my sleep I dreamed, as I lay,
that Afticanus, just in the same array
as Scipio saw him that time before,
just so he came to my bedside and stood.

> 92 But fynally my spirit, at the laste,
> 93 For wery of my labour al the day,
> 94 Tok reste, that made me to slepe faste;
> 9S And in my slep I mette, as that I lay,
> 96 How Affrican, ryght in the selve aray
> 97 That Scipion hym say byfore that tyde,
> 98 Was come and stod right at my beddes syde.

The weary hunter, asleep in his bed,
dreams that he never left the wood;
the judge dreams that his case moves forward;
in the carter's dreams, the cart rolls on;
the rich dream of gold; the knight fights foes;
the sick man dreams he drinks of the cask;
the lover dreams he has his lady won.

> 99 The wery huntere, slepynge in his bed,
> 100 To wode ayeyn his mynde goth anon;
> 101 The juge dremeth how his plees been sped;
> 102 The cartere dremeth how his cart is gon;
> 103 The riche, of gold; the knyght fyght with his fon;
> 104 The syke met he drynketh of the tonne;
> 105 The lovere met he hath his lady wonne.

Can I not say but that the cause of this
was that I had read of Africanus,
and that's what made me dream he stood there.
But what he said: "You've borne yourself well.
You found me in that tattered book —
found me despite the footnotes of Macrobius,
a monk who understood me not at all.
Let me repay your labor with something ... "

    106 Can I not seyn if that the cause were
    107 For I had red of Affrican byforn,
    108 That madde me to mete that he stod there;
    109 But thus seyde he, "Thou hast the so wel born
    110 In lokynge of myn olde bok totorn,
    111 Of which Macrobye roughte nat a lyte,
    112 That somdel of thy labour wolde I quyte" —

Venus! Cytherea, thou blissful lady sweet,
who with your fire-brand conquers
whom you please, you who made me dream this very vision,
be thou my help in this, for you lead best,
as truly as the sail turns north-north-west,
so as I begin my vision to write,
so give me strength to rhyme and indite!

    113 Citherea! thou blysful lady swete,
    114 That with thy fyrbrond dauntest whom the lest,
    115 And madest me this sweven for to mete,
    116 Be thow myn helpe in this, for thow mayst best!
    117 As wisly as I sey the north-north-west,
    118 When I began my sweven for to write,
    119 So yif me myght to ryme, and endyte!

The Middle English text is that published in *The Riverside Chaucer.* "The Dream of Scipio,", translated by Michael Grant, from *Cicero: On the Good Life.*

# ABOUT THE POEMS

I moved to Pittsburgh, Pennsylvania in mid-2015, and commenced my "retirement" there at the beginning of 2016. I described my return to my native region as a two-year living and writing experiment. Could I live well on my truncated income, with all my time free for writing projects, and to continue to operate The Poet's Press and Yogh & Thorn Books? The present volume is the poetic result of that experiment. Readers will give me the "report card" on whether my time was well spent. During these two years I have also re-issued both of my novels with Crossroads Press; published a revised edition of my 2005 poetry collection, *The Gods As They Are, On Their Planets*, a tenth anniversary expanded edition of *Things Seen in Graveyards*, and the second volume of the anthology *Tales of Terror: The Supernatural Poem Since 1800*. Completing the posthumous four-volume edition of the poems and fiction of Emilie Glen was another project in these two years, as well as the posthumous sonnet collection by Jack Veasey. Other Poet's Press projects which had been in the pipeline were finished as well, bringing the press's output to 235 editions.

I wish there had been more new poems, but, like many friends in the arts, I have found events during and since the 2016 U.S. election to be profoundly depressing. Months passed in which I wrote nothing; the crisis has not passed, but my gloom has. All we can do is keep on doing what we do.

The following are brief notes about the poems, essentially what I might say about a poem before reading it aloud, or if asked for background by a curious reader.

AUTUMN DRAGGED SCREAMING continues the 40-plus-year cycle of autumn poems that I have collected as *Anniversarius: The Book of Autumn*. My first fall in Pittsburgh didn't seem fall-like, and this was the first new poem I read here at an open reading.

IN CHILL NOVEMBER is a revision of another poem in the *Anniversarius* cycle. It was written during a train ride in New England, on a late autumn day. I reflected that since everything looked equally dead in the landscape, there was no way to tell, at a distance, the difference between a dead tree and once which had merely shed its leaves.

AUTUMN OF THE OLIGARCHS is the newest of the autumnals, and reflects my darkest thoughts about where our politics are taking us. With the prospects of war and climate-change disaster, the poem might well reflect the secret plans of some very rich, and sociopathic, old men.

ARABESQUES ON THE STATUE OF LIBERTY is a revision of a New York poem. Seeing an angry man on the Staten Island Ferry, staring with hatred at the Statue of Liberty, and then seeing, on Canal Street in Chinatown, a Chinese lady walking with a determined gait holding a miniature of Liberty, prompted this fantasy.

AT THE TOMB OF LEONARDO DA VINCI was inspired by the reading of several biographies of the artist, as well as my study of how the artist's bones (or someone's bones) came to be in France, and not in Italy. After da Vinci's death, his assistant Melzi held onto the master's drawings and notebooks for half a century before the pages were cut up for the drawings, with as much as half the writings lost forever.

THE EXHUMATION OF GOETHE is a revision, recounting the attempt by the East German authorities to unearth Germany's greatest poet and make a public display of them, the Teutonic answer to Lenin's mummy in Red Square. I do not make these things up.

THE MIDNIGHT WALKS OF EBEN BYERS is based on Pittsburgh history, mostly from newspaper accounts of the strange death, and even stranger burial, of a millionaire steel heir who drank 1,400 bottles of radioactive water.

THE ISOLATE STONE describes a lonely grave marker in the North Burial Ground in Providence, Rhode Island. The story of poor Mary is speculative.

THE DRESSER IN EMILY'S BEDROOM. One of my last outings before leaving New England was to make a pilgrimage, with my friends Alexia Kosmider and Tamara Bolotow, to the home of Emily Dickinson in Amherst. Although I had studied Dickinson's poems, most notably in an electrifying graduate class with Mary Cappello, I was not prepared for my reaction to being in the room where Emily died, and where her 18,000 poems were found in a dresser drawer. The *ouija* board, the telegraph, and the slave-ship add hints of the material and cultural outer world beyond Emily's bedroom.

ONE NIGHT IN CYPRUS is one of those poems that waited many years to reach pen and paper. I had the dream which it relates in 1974, and identified the connection of my dream with Archbishop Makarios within a day of its occurrence. Only recently did I read some books on Cyprus, starting with Lawrence Durrell's memoir, *Bitter Lemons*, and proceeding to some histories. I did not appreciate, until that reading, what a significant, and courageous, leader Makarios was. Some would dismiss an experience like this out of hand: all I can say is that it happened, and that I knew, even while dreaming, that these events were happening to someone else at that moment.

DEAD PRINCESS was my response to reading about the London public's response to Princess Diana's death, and the Greek-temple setting of her final resting place.

SNOFRU THE MAD is a revision. This poem is based on my reading about the Pharaoh's life in Gardiner's *History of Ancient Egypt*. When Gardiner noted the "unpalatable" thought that Snofru had built four pyramids, the whole idea of this poem sprang forth in my mind. The historical details are correct, but I have invented the mad Pharaoh's reasoning.

MRS. FRIEDMAN'S GOLEM is a fantasy, but based on actual persons and events in my childhood in Scottdale, Pennsylvania. It includes allusions to a Ku Klux Klan gathering there, a riotous gathering of some 30,000 Klan members, met by armed Catholics who resisted them. How much of this story is true? It was unveiled to me in two dreams, a mix of exact memory and fantasy. The Rabbi, if he existed, must be dead now, so who knows? Was he there? Did he offer to make a Golem? Did he recruit me to help in an attempt to make a Golem? Did he succeed? Did I stare into the eyes of the Golem?

CRACKERS AT MIDNIGHT took place at my grandmother's house outside Scottdale, Pennsylvania. It was a four-room house covered only with black tar-paper, with an outhouse and no running water. I spent some of my childhood summers there.

NIGHT WALKER, a revision, describes an incident in the cemetery at West Newton, Pennsylvania, where I spent four high-school years. It is a true story.

ELDORADO has been rewritten or revised a number of times. It evokes Poe's poem of that title but chooses the glacial kettle lake at Edinboro, Pennsylvania as its locale. The meaning of this poem eludes me. I keep returning to it. Perhaps it is not yet given to me to put it in its final form.

NEW YEAR'S DAY is an actual incident from my high-school years. Dinners in that house were that dreadful, a place that dripped misery to the last floor-board.

THE OWL. I returned to Edinboro, Pennsylvania many times over the years, to visit friends at Edinboro State College (now Edinboro University of Pennsylvania). A mentor who took a kindly interest in me was Dr. Benjamin Lowenhaupt, a biology professor there. This poem recounts a summer visit to his beautiful farm outside Cambridge Springs, PA.

TABLEAUX FROM A PENNSYLVANIA VILLAGE is a revision of a set of four nature poems from 1973. The originals were not much more than journal notes of visual impressions, although the third poem was always cast as a battle between lake and the vegetation around it.

The locale is Edinboro, its beautiful glacial lake, and its maple-lined pioneer graveyard.

LETHE was first written around 1987, and was revised later after I read of the death of actor River Phoenix of a drug overdose. I never was much of a Hippie, as you can read from this tirade against drug addiction deaths. There is nothing romantic about being left behind when someone you love or admire does this to himself. The Juggernaut is a great stone wheel under which Hindu worshippers immolate themselves, an apocryphal story known in English since the 14th century, about the Hindu temple cars of Jagannath Temple in Puri.

MOTHERHOOD relates something seen in a YouTube video. Sad to say, it is almost word-for-word.

WARTIME FRAGMENT is a shard of political gloom.

NERO AND THE FLAMINGO is based on an incident related in Suetonius's *De Vita Caesarum*.

DREAMERS is a sharp response to the threats to the DACA "Dreamers."

WHO CAN BE A POET ALL OF THE TIME? is a revised version that makes even clearer than before the gulf between poets who are called to be poets, no matter what, as opposed to the careerists of the "poetry guild." The general rottenness of the poetry world has been widely written about, so I need not belabor it.

SWAN LAKE VARIATIONS won't mean much to those who have never seen Tchaikovsky's ballet. In the first part, I paraphrase twelve different alternate endings that various choreographers have devised. In the second part, I comment on the 2018 production in Pittsburgh, which featured a happy ending. To me, a *Swan Lake* that does not end in death and desolation is no *Swan Lake* at all.

LINES OVERHEARD IN THE RUSSIAN TEA ROOM is satire. At the original Russian Tea Room, the tables were so close together that one always heard snippets of all the conversations at adjacent tables. For those born too recently, "Moose and Squirrel" refers to the popular 1960s animated cartoon show, *Rocky the Flying Squirrel and Bullwinkle the Moose*, which featured inept Russian spies.

VARIATIONS ON THE IBIS was a poem that waited a long time to get to paper. I have owned the ibis painting by Riva Leviten for years, and always wanted to relate the sparks of visual-poetic recognition that passed magically between us when we we near-neighbors in Providence, Rhode Island. Then, in 2017, I came upon the appalling description of the habits of the ibis in Peter Green's majestic history, *Alexander to Actium: The Historical Evolution of the Hellenistic Age*. This provoked joining the mystical fascination with the ibis, to the stark biology of the scavenger bird, as two radically different variations.

THE COMPANY OF AN EAGLE is a radical rewrite of an older poem. The surrealist paintings of René Magritte showing a mountain in the form of an eagle, with an egg in the foreground (*The Domain of Arnheim*, 1938, 1947), was one direct provocation. Back in the 1970s, poet Barbara A. Holland and I used to regale one another with Magritte-inspired poems. Most, like this, were a first-person narrative or complaint, so that the ekphrastic (art-descriptive) joins the narrative. Anyone who has had a date with a distracted/married man, will get the gist of this.

FRONTIER and THWARTED are rewrites of old poems from the 1970s. I clearly didn't have much fun in the 1970s.

PLEASE, NO begins as an account of my one-and-only "Jackie O" sighting, but then it takes an unexpected turn.

WOOING is an adaptation from the Latin of Martial.

THE LOVED DEAD is revised from the 1970s. The poem NECROPOLIS was a 2017 addition, but then I split it off as a separate poem. Although the phrase "loved dead" recurs in the second poem, each poem is about a different person, and I felt it to be awkward to have them under one title. So think of them as two takes on the same idea. With the HIV/AIDS epidemic, many in my generation live in a haunted landscape with constant reminders of our departed friends and loved ones.

POETS IN A CHELSEA BROWNSTONE is a memory from my many years in the Manhattan poetry scene. Marion Tanner was the inspiration for her nephew Patrick Dennis' best-selling novel-memoir, *Auntie Mame*, the basis in turn of a Broadway play and an Oscar-winning film, and then a Broadway musical, and finally a film of that musical.

PROLOGUE TO CHAUCER'S PARLIAMENT OF FOWLES is a quick translation that I did while studying Chaucer with University of Rhode Island professor Walter Cane. Walter died in 2017, but his warm humanist teaching of Shakespeare and Chaucer remains with all his students. It is combined with a little bit of Cicero's *Dream of Scipio* to make the poem more self-explicating.

— BRETT RUTHERFORD
*Pittsburgh, Pennsylvania*
*March 1, 2018*

# ABOUT THE POET

Brett Rutherford, born in Scottdale, Pennsylvania, began writing poetry seriously during a stay in San Francisco. During his college years at Edinboro State College in Pennsylvania, he published an underground newspaper and printed his first hand-made poetry chapbook. He moved to New York City, where he founded The Poet's Press in 1971. For more than twenty years, he worked as an editor, journalist, printer, and consultant to publishers and nonprofit organizations.

After a literary pilgrimage to Providence, Rhode Island, on the track of H.P. Lovecraft and Edgar Allan Poe, he moved there with his press. *Poems From Providence* was the fruit of his first three years in the city (1985-1988), published in 1991. Since then, he has written a study of Edgar Allan Poe and Providence poet Sarah Helen Whitman (briefly Poe's fiancee), a biographical play about Lovecraft, and his second novel, *The Lost Children* (Zebra Books, 1988). His poetry, in volumes both thematic and chronological, can be found in *Poems From Providence* (1991, 2011), *Things Seen in Graveyards* (2007), *Twilight of the Dictators* (1992, 2009), *The Gods As They Are, On their Planets* (2005, 2012), *Whippoorwill Road: The Supernatural Poems* (1998, 2005, 2012), and *An Expectation of Presences* (2012).

Returning to school for a master's degree in English, Rutherford completed this project in 2007, and worked for University of Rhode Island in distance learning, and taught for the Gender and Women's Studies Department. There, he created courses on "The Diva," "Women in Science Fiction," and "Radical American Women."

He has prepared annotated editions of Matthew Gregory Lewis's *Tales of Wonder*, the poetry of Charles Hamilton Sorley, A.T. Fitzroy's antiwar novel *Despised and Rejected*, and the four-volume collected writings of Emilie Glen.

His interests include classical music and opera, and Latin American music; Chinese art, history and literature; bicycling, graveyards, woods, horror films, intellectual history, and crimes against nature.

Retiring from his workaday life in early 2016, Rutherford moved to the Squirrel Hill neighborhood in Pittsburgh where he continues to write, to study music, and to run The Poet's Press.

# ABOUT THIS BOOK

The body text for this book is Plantin. Several attractive modern fonts, including Galliard and Plantin, are based on typefaces originally designed by Robert Granjon (1513-1589), a prolific type designer and founder active in Paris, in the shop of Christoph Plantin, and later in Rome at the Vatican. In 1913, Monotype issued several versions of Plantin, based on some of Granjon's designs. Section and main titles are set in Solemnis, a calligraphic font designed in 1953 by Günter Gerhard Lange for the Berthold Foundry. Poem titles are set in Schneidler Black. The book is also decorated with several 18$^{th}$-century Dutch borders and ornaments.

The illustrations for this book are mostly photographs and digital art from photographs by the author. The Ibis painting is a watercolor by Riva Leviten, from the author's collection. "In the Company of An Eagle" is derived from a low-resolution photograph of Magritte's 1947 canvas, *The Domain of Arnheim*.

www.ingramcontent.com/pod-product-compliance
Lightning Source LLC
Chambersburg PA
CBHW051655040426
42446CB00009B/1151